THE
RACES OF AFGHANISTAN

THE
RACES OF AFGHANISTAN,

BEING

A BRIEF ACCOUNT OF THE PRINCIPAL NATIONS INHABITING THAT COUNTRY.

BY
SURGEON-MAJOR H. W. BELLEW, C.S.I.,
LATE ON SPECIAL POLITICAL DUTY AT KABUL

GYAN

Published by

Gyan Publishing House
5, Ansari Road
Daryaganj, New Delhi-110002
Phone: 011-47034999, 9811692060
E-mail: books@gyanbooks.com

Distribution Network
gyanbooks.com
India, USA, Canada, UK, Australia, France

ISBN : 978-81-212-3931-8 (PB)
First Published, 1880

2nd Impression 2020

Printed at: Gyan Press, Delhi.

The Races of Afghanistan
Author: Surgeon Major H. W. Bellew

THE

RACES OF AFGHANISTAN,

BEING

A BRIEF ACCOUNT OF THE PRINCIPAL NATIONS INHABITING THAT COUNTRY.

BY

SURGEON-MAJOR H. W. BELLEW, C.S.I.,
LATE ON SPECIAL POLITICAL DUTY AT KABUL.

CALCUTTA:
THACKER, SPINK, AND CO.

1880.

CONTENTS.

PREFACE.

THE manuscript of the following brief account of the races of Afghanistan was written at Kabul, for the most part, after the duties of the day were over, and at odd intervals of leisure from official business, with the view to its transmission to England for publication; but falling ill as it drew to a close, and being obliged on that account to leave Kabul for India on sick leave, my purpose could not be carried out.

And now, on arrival in India, finding myself unable to revise the text, or enlarge it, as I should wish to do, by the introduction of much useful and interesting matter which is available, I have thought it advisable to bring the work to the notice of the public without further delay, rather than indefinitely postpone its appearance to an uncertain future. And likewise, fully sensible as I am of the incompleteness of the work and its shortcomings, still, as events are progressing with rapid strides in the country with whose peoples it deals, and it is of importance that the subject should be early brought to the notice of the thinking public, I have deemed it preferable to let the book go forth in its incompleteness, in the hope that it may direct attention and further enquiry and research into the national peculiarities of the several races treated of; since I believe that, for the peace and security of our Indian Empire, they must, ere very long, be enrolled among the list of its various subjects; and this, by the force of impelling and unavoidable circumstances. For, to know the history, interests, and aspirations of a people, is half the battle gained in converting them to loyal, contented, and peaceable subjects, to willing participators and active protectors of the welfare of the Empire towards which, from position and self-interest, they naturally gravitate.

H. W. B.

LAHORE;
29th January, 1880.

THE RACES OF AFGHANISTAN.

CHAPTER I.

INTRODUCTORY.

Now that our armies are in possession of Kandahar and Kabul—the earlier and later capitals, respectively, of the lapsed Durrani Empire, and, as regards the latter, the seat of government of the succeeding Durrani Rulers, that is to say, the capitals of the Saddozai Shahs and Barakzai Amirs—the question arises, what are we to do with the country heretofore governed from these seats of authority, and latterly in the possession of the Ruler seated at Kabul.

The question is one which must before very long be answered by the logic of accomplished facts, consequent on the stern demands of necessity more than of mere policy. For having, as we have now done, completely destroyed the authority and government of the tyrannous and treacherous Durrani Rulers, whose power it has been our policy to maintain and strengthen during the past quarter of a century, it is now incredible that we shall deliberately abandon the vantage ground gained, ignore the great danger we have now thereby staved off, and leave the country a prey to internal anarchy, and a prize to the first external adventurer. It is equally incomprehensible that we should again commit the folly of restoring the destroyed government of the Amirs—

of rulers who have successively proved themselves faithless to their engagements, treacherous in their dealings, and hostile in their conduct towards the British Government. The other alternative is to administer the country ourselves, either directly, or through the medium of native agency under our own supervision. And in the belief that this is the responsibility which we must sooner or later take upon ourselves, I venture to offer to the notice of the public the following brief account of the principal nations inhabiting Afghanistan, by way of a small contribution towards properly understanding their several tribes and their diverse national interests and political tendencies.

The political measures initiated at Simla before our avenging army crossed the border on its righteous errand, and which brought the Durrani Amir into the British camp and placed his capital in the hands of the British General—and this without opposition, for the demonstration made at Charasya on the 6th October by a hastily collected rabble is not to be seriously considered in the light of an effort to defend the city—put us in possession, without serious resistance, of not only the person of the Amir, but of his vast stores of military munitions—guns by the hundred, rifles by the thousand, cartridges by the million, and powder by the ton. In fact, by our unopposed march to Kabul we knocked down what we had built up—the power of the Amir over a consolidated kingdom; and we destroyed what we had helped to create—vast stores of war material.

And all this not a moment too soon. For we now know for a certainty, what was only suspected before, that the one was nurtured in the deepest treachery to his publicly pledged alliance and friendship, and that the other was diligently increased from day to day for the opportunity to be expended against us. But it is not my object in these pages to discuss this subject, nor yet the conduct of our operations in Afghanistan. These topics can be more conveniently and advantageously dealt with hereafter, when the history of the present and preceding campaigns in this country comes to be written as the final issue of a quarter of a century of political relations with the Durrani rulers of Afghanistan.

It is more to our present purpose to consider who the people are with whom, under the comprehensive term Afghan, we are now brought into direct contact, and whom it will ere very long be our inevitable duty to govern as subjects of our Indian Empire. Of the necessity of this issue of our past and present dealings with this country there is no longer any advantage in blinking the conviction. And the sooner we declare our will, the more promptly will the people accept the situation, and accommodate themselves to the new regime of British rule, justice, and protection.

In the composition of the Afghan nation there are many conditions favourable and advantageous to the peaceable and secure establishment of our rule, if we only set about the work with earnest and intelligent purpose. And the due appreciation of these conditions will be the crucial test of our success or failure.

As an aid towards arriving at a correct judgment on this all-important question, an enquiry into the origin and ethnic affinities of the various peoples composing the complex Afghan nationality—apart from the inherent interest of the subject itself—may perhaps at the present juncture prove useful. The enquiry will at the same time make clear to the reader the prime causes of the anarchy and instability which have characterized the history of the country ever since it emerged from a position of subordination to its neighbouring empires on the side of Persia and India respectively, to one of absolute independence under native sovereigns—causes which owe their origin to the diversity of race and the antagonism of tribal interests among a heterogeneous and barbarous people, who have been only brought together as a nationality by the accident of position and the bond of a common religion.

Before entering upon this enquiry, it is necessary to premise—less as a hint to the captious critic than as an apology to the earnest student—that the work has been written for the most part from memory at odd intervals of leisure from official duties during the course of the present campaign in Kabul, and, with the exception of some note-book memoranda which I happened to have at hand, without the means of reference to authorities for dates and details. The account is, therefore, necessarily of a brief and summary nature; but such as it is, however, I trust that it will be found to embody sufficient information—much of which is entirely new, and, so far as I am aware, now for the first time published, being the result of personal enquiries and research during several years' service on the Afghan Frontier—to enable the general reader to understand the mutual relations towards each other and towards ourselves of the several distinct peoples comprised in what is known to us as the Afghan nationality.

For the purposes of this enquiry it will suffice to consider as Afghanistan all that region which is bounded on the north by the Oxus, and on the south by Balochistan; on the east by the middle course of the Indus, and on the west by the desert of Persia. The inhabitants of the area thus defined are not a united nation of the same stock and lineage; nor do they possess the same political interests and tribal affinities. On the contrary, they consist of different races, and diverse nationalities, with rival interests and antagonistic ambitions as towards each other.

The only common bond of union among them is that of religion, and to this their devotion is of a fanatic kind, owing to the blindness of their ignorance and the general barbarism of their social condition. It is a devotion, too, which has been fostered and stimulated in no small degree—though not always with uniform earnestness of response—through the priesthood by the persistent and determined efforts of the dominant race,—of the Durrani,—who has owed the continuance of his authority and power to our consistent support in return for a pledged friendship which has at last been discovered to the world as false and treacherous from beginning to end.

The cohesion, however, which the several distinct races derive from the influence of a common religion is not very strong nor very durable, owing to the classification, somewhat unequal though it be, of the people under the two great and hostile sects into which the church of Muhammad, known by the term Islam (whence Muslim, plural Muslimin, *vulgo* Musalmán, the name for its professors), is divided. In other words, owing to their division into the orthodox Sunni and the heterodox Shia. So great and so irreconcilable are the jealousies and animosities of these two rival sects, that they destroy, to a considerable extent, the strength otherwise derivable from the profession of a common religion. And thus it is we find that the religious element alone fails completely to dominate the divergencies of race instincts and tribal interests.

To the operation of these causes combined is to be attributed the fact that the Afghan nationality remains a disunited agglomeration of different races, which are only loosely held together, so long as one or other of them, propped by external alliance and support, is maintained in a position of dominance as the ruling race. For the last hundred and thirty years, more or less, this dominant position has been held by the Afghan, or, as he is generally styled in reference to his being of the ruling race, the Durrani; and it is from him that the complex nationality, as well as the country itself, have received their names—Afghan and Afghanistan.

The principal nationalities which together compose the inhabitants of Afghanistan, are the Afghan, the Pathán, the Ghilzai, the Tájik, and the Hazarah. There are besides the lesser nationalities of the Chár Aymác on the western frontiers about Herat, the Uzbak on the southern bank of the Oxus, and the Kafir on the southern slopes of Hindu Kush. These, however, exercise little, if any, influence in the affairs of the country as a whole, and need not now engage our attention. Let us proceed to notice as briefly as possible each of the first set in turn.

CHAPTER II.

THE AFGHAN.

THE traditions of this people refer them to Syria as the country of their residence at the time they were carried away into captivity by Bukhtunasar (Nebuchadnezzar), and planted as colonists in different parts of Persia and Media. From these positions they, at some subsequent period, emigrated eastward into the mountainous country of Ghor, where they were called by the neighbouring peoples "Bani Afghan" and "Bani Israíl," or children of Afghan and children of Israel In corroboration of this we have the testimony of the prophet Esdras to the effect that the ten tribes of Israel, who were carried into captivity, subsequently escaped and found refuge in the country of Arsareth, which is supposed to be identical with the Hazarah country of the present day, and of which Ghor forms a part. It is also stated in the Tabacati Nasiri—a historical work which contains, among other information, a detailed account of the conquest of this country by Changhiz Khan—that in the time of the native Shansabi dynasty there was a people called Bani Israíl living in that country, and that some of them were extensively engaged in trade with the countries around.

This people was settled in the Ghor country, to the east of Herat, at the time that Muhammad announced his mission as the Prophet of God—about 622 A. D. And it was there that Khalid-bin-Walíd, a chief of the Curesh tribe of Arabs, came to them with the tidings of the new faith, and an invitation to join the Prophet's standard. The errand of this Arab apostle would apparently support the view held by some that the Afghan people were originally of an Arab tribe, and had linked their fortunes with the Israelites in Syria, and shared the lot of the ten tribes which were carried away into captivity. Be this as it may, the mission of Khalid was not without success, for he returned to the Prophet, accompanied by a deputation of six or seven representative men of the Afghan people and their followers amounting in all to seventy-six persons. The chief or leader of this party was named Kais or Kish.

The traditions of the people go on to the effect that this Kais and his companions fought so well and successfully in the cause of the Prophet, that Muhammad, on dismissing them to their homes, presented them with handsome gifts, complimented them on their bravery, and giving them his blessing foretold a glorious career for their nation, and promised that the title of Malik (or king) should distinguish their chiefs for ever. (The term "Malik," it may be here noted, is apparently peculiar to the Afghan nationality. At the present day it is the title of the lowest grade of nobility among the Afghan, the Pathán, and the Ghilzai,—that is to say, the Pukhto-speaking races. Among the Persian-speaking races, the corresponding term is "Kalántar" among the Tájik, and "Mihtar" among the Hazarah, and Acsacál among the Turk tribes of Balkh. In each case the term signifies "chief" or "elder.") At the same time the Prophet, as a mark of special favour and distinction, was pleased to change the Hebrew name of Kais to the Arab one of Abdur Rashíd—"the servant of the true guide"—and, exhorting him to strive in the conversion of his people, conferred on him the title of "Pahtán,"—a term which the Afghan book-makers explain to be a Syrian word signifying the rudder of a ship, as the new proselyte was henceforth to be the guide of his people in the way they should go.

For centuries after this period the history of the Afghans as a distinct people is involved in much obscurity, and it would seem that it was only some three or four hundred years ago that their priests began concocting genealogies and histories to give form and cohesion to the very mixed nationality which had at about that time grown into existence as a result of the political convulsions and dynastic revolutions, which during preceding centuries had jumbled up together within the area of the country now known as Afghanistan a variety of different races, some of which were original or early occupants, and others new-comers.

At what period the Afghans of Ghor moved forward and settled in the Kandahar country, which is now their home, is not known. It appears, however, from the writings of the early Muhammadan historians, that in the first century of their era—the seventh-eighth of ours—the province of Sistan was occupied by an Indian people. At that time the territorial extent of Sistan was very much wider than the restricted little province of the present day. At that time Sistan, or Sajistan as it is written in native books, comprised all the country from the head waters of the Tarnak and Arghasan rivers and the Toba range of hills on the east, to the Nih Bandán range of hills and Dashti Náummed—Desert of Despair—on the west; from the valleys of the Helmand and Arghandáb rivers on the north, to the Khoja Amrán range and the Balochistan desert on the south. It comprised, in fact, the Drangiana and Arachósia of the Greek writers. The former was afterwards called Sijistan after the Saka Scythians, who occupied it about the first century of our era, and the latter was called Gandhár after the Indian Gandhára, who, it seems, overpowered a kindred people in prior possession some time after the Greek conquest.

Who the Indian people occupying this country at the time of this Arab invasion were will be mentioned presently, but it seems clear they were not the only inhabitants thereof, but shared it with the native Persian and other immigrant tribes of Scythic origin. For the province itself derived its name of Sákistán, Sagistan, Sajistán, Sístán from the Sáka, who were probably the same people as the Sáká Hámuvarga mentioned in the tables of Darius (see Rawlinson's Herodotus) —"Şáká dwellers on the Hámú" or Amú, which has from the earliest times been the name of the lower course of the Oxus river; the latter term being the Greek form of Wakhsh, which is the name of the Upper Oxus above the point where it is joined by the Panjah.

It is probable that, in the course of the repeated military expeditions carried by the Arabs from the side of Persia against Sind, a variety of new races were brought into the country forming the southern part of the present Afghanistan, and that extensive changes occurred in the previously existing local distribution of the inhabitants. In the beginning of the tenth century of our era, the country of Zábulistán (the old name of the southern half of Afghanistan, as Kábulistán was of its northern half) was inhabited by a variety of races speaking different languages, and even at that time the Arab writers were puzzled as to their origin and identification.

This being so, we may conclude that the Afghans when they advanced into Kandahar, which they did in all probability as military colonists under the standard of the Arab Khálif, at first held their own by force of arms, but gradually being in the minority as to numbers, blended with the conquered people, and became absorbed in the general population of the country. As conquerors, however, they retained their own national title, which in time became that of the conquered people with whom, by intermarriage, they identified themselves. This view is supported by the evidence afforded by their genealogical tables, which, it appears, were only concocted long centuries after the Arab conquest of the country, and the conversion of its heterogeneous population to the new faith which so rapidly spread over and changed the face of Asia.

The fictions of the Afghan genealogists and historians are absurd enough, and their facts wonderfully distorted; but for the careful enquirer they have their value as guides to a right conclusion. Thus, from the Kais above-mentioned, whose own tribe was originally but an insignificant people as to numbers and power, the Afghan genealogists derive all the Pukhto-speaking peoples of Afghanistan, partly by direct descent, and partly by adoption on account of a similarity of language and social polity.

Kais, they say, married a daughter of that Khalid-bin-Walíd who brought his people the first tidings of the Prophet and his doctrine, and by her he had three sons, whom he named respectively, Saraban, Batan, and Ghurghusht. These names are of themselves very remarkable, and at once afford a clue to the composition of the nation from an ethnic point of view, as will be seen in the further course of this treatise.

The Afghans Proper—the Bani Israíl, as they call themselves in special distinction to all other divisions of the nation—class themselves as the descendants of Saraban through his two sons, Sharjyún and Khrishyún. From Sharjyún there sprung five clans, the principal of which is called Sheoráni. From Khrishyún there sprung three clans, namely, Kand, Zamand, and Kansí. The Kand was divided into the Khakhí and Ghorí, and included the Mandanr and Yúsufzai clans. They are all now settled in the Peshawar valley.

The ZAMAND were originally settled on the lower course of the Arghasán river and in Peshín or Foshang, as it was at that time—8-9 H. or 630 A. D.—called. They were subsequently ousted by the Tarín tribe of Afghans, and emigrated to Multan in large numbers. But their chief clan, called Khúshgí or Khushgari, emigrated by way of Ghazni and Kabul to the Ghorband and adjoining valleys of Hindu Kush, and settled there. In the time of the Emperor Babur, most of them accompanied his armies into India, and there founded a settlement at Kasúr near Lahore. Some of them remained in the Peshawar valley, where the village of Khweshgi marks their principal settlement. There are still many of the clan in Ghorband and Kohistan of Kabul, where they are now known by the name of Khúshkári or Kúchkárí.

The KANSI early emigrated to Hindustan and the Dekkan, and are not now known in Afghanistan, though by some the Shinwári are supposed to belong to this division.

These several tribes are divided into a number of clans and sub-tribes, the names of many of which are distinctly of Indian origin. The special Afghan tribe, however, is called Abdálí, and is more commonly known since the time of Ahmad Shah—the first independent sovereign of Afghanistan of this race—by the name Durrani. The Durrani comprise the following chief divisions or clans, namely, Saddozai, Populzai, Bárakzai, Halakozai, Achakzai, Núrzai, Isháczai, and Khágwání. Their home and fixed seat is Kandahar province—the former country of the Gandhára, who, at an early period of our era, spread into the present Hazarah country along the courses of the Helmand and Arghandáb rivers. Members of each clan, however, are found in small societies scattered all over the plain country up to Kabul and Jalalabad, and they are there settled mostly as lords of the soil or military feoffees, the people of the country, so far as concerns the agricultural community, being their tenants or serfs.

The SADDOZAI clan furnished the first independent Shahs, or kings, of the Durrani dynasty, and the Bárakzai furnished the Amirs, or dictators. The line of the Shahs was overthrown in the third generation, after a protracted period of anarchy and contention which broke out immediately after the death of the first king and founder of the national independence. The line of the Amirs, entirely owing to the consistent support of the British Government, has reached a fourth successor in the person of the now evilly notorious Yacúb Khan.

We must now return to the ancestor, among whose descendants the Afghans class themselves, namely, Sáraban. This name is evidently a corruption, or perhaps a natural variant form of Suryabans—the solar or royal race—now represented in India by the Rájpút. Similarly the names of his sons Khrishyún and Sharjyún, and of his grandson Sheoráni, are clearly changed forms of the common Rájpút and Brahman proper names Krishan, Surjan, and Shivaram or Sheoram.

How the Afghan genealogy-mongers came to adopt the name Saraban will be understood, if we refer to the anterior history of the country in which that people settled as conquerors. It was stated in a preceding passage that, during the first century of the Muhammadan era—the seventh of our own—the country of Sistan, which at that time included the present province of Kandahar, was inhabited by an Indian people, whom it was the persistent effort of the Arabs to conquer and convert. And we know from the records of history that, apart from the transfer or displacement of populations consequent upon prior irruptions of Scythic hordes from the north-east, there took place about two centuries earlier, or during the fifth and beginning of the sixth of our era, a very powerful emigration of an Indian people from the western bank of the Indus to the valley of the Helmand and its tributary streams, towards a kindred people already settled there.

This emigration *en masse* was owing, it would appear, to the irruption into the Indus valley of the Jats, and Katti, and other Scythic tribes, who about that period poured over the Hindu Kush. The Jats and Katti—the Getes and Catti of European authors—are now largely represented in this seat of their early conquest in the Jat (or Gújar as he is commonly styled) agricultural population of the Panjab, and in the Katti of Kattiwar or Kattiyawar.

In Afghanistan the Jat is known by the name of Gújar, which is a Hindi term expressive of his calling as a rearer of cattle and a husbandman, and he is found in the greatest numbers in the Yúsufzai country, especially in the hill districts of Swat, Buner, and Bajáwar.

The KATTI are not known in Afghanistan as a distinct people, though, apparently, they have left a trace of their name in the district of Kattawáz, to the south-east of Ghazni, and in certain sub-divisions of the Ghilzai tribe who bear the names Kuttakhel and Kattikhel.

This body of Indian emigrants, who migrated from the Indus to the Helmand, was composed of a people professing the Budhist religion, and who, fleeing away from the irresistible wave of Scythic invasion, abandoned their native country, and took along with them the most sacred and cherished relic of their spiritual lawgiver—the water-pot of Budha. The relic, which is a huge bowl carved out of a solid block of dark green serpentine, when I saw it in 1872—and most likely it is still in the same position—was lying in an obscure little Muhammadan shrine, only a few hundred paces distant from the ruins of Kuhna Shahr—" old city"—ancient Kandahar. The descendants of the Budhists who carried it there have long since become Musalmáns, and merged their identity in the common brotherhood of Islám. The sacred relic of the faith of their ancestors, unrecognized and uncared for, is now covered with Arabic inscriptions, and lies neglected and forgotten in an obscure corner close to the spot where it was in times gone by treated with the utmost reverence and most pious care. Its history is forgotten, and, like that of the infidels connected with it, is an utter blank to the fanatic Musalmán of the present day. It is enough for the people that they enjoy the blessing of being counted among " The Faithful," and bear the glorious name of Afghan. So powerful is the effect of Islám, in effacing class distinctions and ancient memorials, to reduce all its professors to a common brotherhood in the faith.

The Indian people who emigrated from the Indus and established themselves as a powerful colony on the Helmand were the Gandarii, and their country was the Gandaria of the Greek authors. They were the Gandhárí, and their country the Sindhú Gandhára of the Hindu writers. This people and their country will be noticed more fully hereafter, but it may be stated here that the early emigrants not only gave the name of Gandhár, or Kandhár, or Kandahár to the prime seat of their new settlement and rule, but actually, some ten centuries later, sent a powerful colony back to their primitive home. Return emigrants entirely ignorant of their mother country, and, regenerated by Islám, treating their kindred and foreigners alike, without distinction, as cursed infidels and "Hindus."

The emigration of the Yúsufzai and Mahmand, with the Khakhí and Ghoryákhel Afghans from the Kandahar province to the Peshawar valley, will be described further on. Here it will suffice to indicate the reason why the Afghan genealogist took the term Saraban for the name of the ancestor of the first of the three nations orginally sprung from, or referred to, their great progenitor Kais. Suryabans was the distinctive race title of the Rájpút people among whom the Afghans had become absorbed, and, independently of clan divisions and sub-divisions, it was also a title held in high respect among the people of the country at that time. Further, as it included a large and important population, it was a convenient term to adopt as an ancestral title.

Its adoption, however, in no way tended to keep alive the origin or influence of the term, nor that of the people to whom the titlo specially applied. This, perhaps, was partly owing to the disguised form of the word, but mostly to the levelling influence of the new religion. It appears from a comparison of the national character and customs of the Rájpúts of India and those of Afghanistan, as represented by the Afghan, that there is a very remarkable similarity between the two peoples. As for instance in the laws of hospitality, protection to the refugee, exaction of vengeance, jealousy of female honour, the brother becoming by right husband of his deceased brother's widow, and others which are also ordained by the Mosaic code. As to national character, the warlike spirit and insufferance of control, addiction to vices and debauchery, instability of purpose, pride of race, jealousy of national honour and personal dignity, and spirit of domineering are pretty much alike in the two peoples now parted more by Brahmanism and Muhammadanism than by mere territorial distance. Apart from these again, there is the very striking physiognomic resemblance, which is even more pronouncedly of the Jewish type in the Rájpút of India than it is in his distant kinsman the Afghan.

By Muhammadans of Asia Minor and the Western countries the Afghan is usually called Sulemáni, apparently from the supposition that he dwells on the Sulemán range of mountains. If so, the name is misapplied, for there are no Afghans settled on that range. It would appear more probable that the name is connected with the ancient Solymi of Syria, who are mentioned by Herodotus, and who were in olden times much mixed up with the Israelites in that country. It is not improbable that some of these Solymi were also carried into captivity along with the Israelites, and that they may have become incorporated with that people, and accompanied them in their subsequent wanderings. In this case we might suppose that some of them were among the Afghans of Ghor, and the supposition would explain the mission of Khalid-bin-Walíd to these Afghans, for the Solymi were an Arab people of the same race as Khalid. It is possible, indeed, that the Solymi of the ancients and the Afghan of the moderns, were originally one and the same people, and that the Bani Israíl were merely refugees among them, for, at the time of their first settlement in Ghor, they were always spoken of separately as "Bani Afgháua" and "Bani Isráil."

By the people of India, and of the East generally, the Afghan is more commonly known by the name Pathán, in common with all other Pukhto-speaking peoples. Sometimes he is also called Rohilla, but this name is properly applicable only to the true Patháu, the native of Roh (the Highlands), the true Highlander, as will be explained further on under the head of Patháu. Amongst themselves, and in their own country, the Afghans rarely, if ever, call themselves by these names. They are simply Afghán or Aoghán, as it is commonly pronounced, of such or such a clan; or they are Durrani, a term which only came into use with the rise of the nation to an independent sovereignty under Ahmad Shah in 1747. It is the name, too, by which this people is known in India as representing a distinct government. The Afghans admit that they are Pukhtána—the Hindustani form of which is Pathán—but they are careful in insisting on the distinction between Afghan and Pathán (or Pukhtána, the word in use among themselves). In fact, as they say, every Afghan is a Pukhtún (singular of Pukhtána), but every Pukhtún, or Pathán, is not an Afghan. The distinction thus made is a very proper one, for the two peoples are of different race and origin. The Afghan is a Pathán merely because he inhabits a Pathán country, and has to a great extent mixed with its people, and adopted their language. The people of the country, on their part, have adopted the religion, and with it many of the manners and customs of the Afghans, though most tribes still retain certain ancient customs peculiar to themselves, which have survived their conversion to Islám, and serve as guides to the elucidation of their previous history. To enter upon an investigation of this subject is altogether beyond the scope of this treatise. It is one, however, of absorbing interest, and would well repay the labour of research.

From what has been stated, we see that the Afghans are a distinct and peculiar people among several other peoples, who together compose the mixed population of the country which is now named after them. They call themselves "Bani Israíl," and trace their descent from King Saul (Malik Tálút) in regular succession down to Kais or Kish, the great ancestor of their nation in Afghanistan.

Of their numbers at the present day it is difficult to form an estimate, though I think it probable that they do not exceed a million souls, if even they be so many. They have for many centuries enjoyed a high reputation for their martial qualities, and have been largely employed in the armies of every conqueror invading India from the north-west or west. Numerous colonies and baronies of their people are to be found scattered about in different parts of the Indian peninsula, and they at one time—the thirteenth century—established a dynasty of kings at Dehli. They have risen into real importance, however, only within the last century and a half or so. And this by the accident of their sudden and unexpected bound to independence and the dominant rule of their country. As a people they have always been evilly notorious for their faithlessness, lawlessness, treachery, and brutality, so much so that the saying *Afghán be-imán*—" the Afghan is faithless"—has passed into a proverb among neighbouring peoples, and, oddly enough, is acknowledged by themselves to be a true count, not only in their dealings with the stranger, but among themselves too. So far as their history as an independent and ruling people goes they have certainly not belied the character assigned to them. A darker record of misgovernment, of vice, of treachery, of savage cruelty, and of oppression, than marks the career of the independent Afghans, is hardly to be found in the annals of any other independent state of modern times, or of the same period.

Let us glance at their history from the time they first became known to the world as an independent people under a king of their own race. It is not a long period to go over—only one hundred and thirty-two years—and the review brief and hurried as it must necessarily be, will show what they have done and what they have not done for their country and their compatriots. For most of the facts and dates brought together in the following summary account I am indebted to MacGregor's Gazetteer of Afghanistan—a perfect mine of information regarding that country, its tribes, its history, its geography, &c., &c.

CHAPTER III.

HISTORY OF THE AFGHANS.

At the beginning of the last century Afghanistan, at that time known as Khurasan (a Persian word signifying the East or the Levant of the Persians) was divided pretty equally between the Mughal and the Persian Empires,—that is to say, Kabul and Ghazni pertained to the former, and Herat and Kandahar to the latter. Both empires had for long striven for the possession of the other half, and Kandahar had repeatedly passed from the grasp of one to that of the other.. Both Herat and Kandahar hated the Persian rule, as much on account of the existing differences of race, language, and religion, the one being Sunni and the other Shiá, as on account of proximity and the dread of strict rule; whilst towards the Mughal Empire they looked with feelings of attachment, partly on account of race affinities, partly on account of trade interests, and partly on account of religious unity, and to some extent also on account of distance and the hope of a mild and protective government.

The glory of each empire, however, had long been on the wane; the stability of each was undermined; and each went at its own pace—rapid in the one case, and slower in the other —to final destruction. At the time we commence from, the Ghilzais of Kandahar began to show some impatience of Persian rule, and successive armies were sent to bring them to obedience. The severity of the Persian general and his troops, however, only exasperated the people to more combined resistance, and, in 1707, the Ghilzais rose in open revolt under their chief Mir Wais, who killed the Persian governor and drove his troops from Kandahar, and himself assumed the government as an independent ruler. This act was the match that fired the long prepared train.

Within a short decade, the Afghans of Herat (there commonly called Abdáli) followed the example of Kandahar, and rose in revolt under their chief Asadulla Khan, Saddozai, who ousted the Persian governor, and himself became independent ruler of the province.

And so matters stood in Western Afghanistan till the close of the first quarter of the century.

About this time there appeared on the scene, as General of the Persian army, Nadir, the celebrated Turkman freebooter, who very soon acquired a world-wide notoriety as the ruthless conqueror of both the Persian and Mughal Empires. He ejected the Ghilzais and Afghans, who had in the interim overrun Persia, recovered Herat, drove back the Russians, and then, deposing his sovereign, assumed the crown himself in 1732. Five years later, Nadir Shah took Kandahar after a protracted siege, razed the grand old city to the ground, ploughed up its interior, and built a mean substitute, which he called Nadirabad, on a low swampy site on the plain a mile or so to the eastward. Whilst engaged in the siege of Kandahar, he enlisted a strong force of Ghilzais and Afghans, ravaged the country around, reduced the people to subjection, and finally, on the fall of the city, he advanced to the conquest of Kabul and Northern India. Ten years later again, 1747, the conqueror of the Panjab and the author of the massacre of Delhi was assassinated just as he reached the Persian border laden with untold spoil, renowned as the conqueror of the age, and execrated as the rival of those ruthless scourges—Changhiz and Tymur.

And now we come to the role of the Afghan. On his march to India, Nadir had raised under his standard a strong contingent of Afghans. His plan was this. He ordered a census by households to be taken of every tribe in the country, and then ordered a certain percentage from each to join his standard at appointed places, fully equipped for the field. The enumeration then made is the only existing authority for the population of this country, and is still quoted by the people as the index of the strength of their several tribes.

Among the Afghan troops so raised was an Abdáli noble, chief of the Saddozai tribe. His name was Ahmad Khan, and he joined the conqueror's standard with a contingent of 10,000 horse. On the return march from India, Ahmad Khan himself with a weak detachment of his men was in attendance in the royal camp, the bulk of his contingent being in rear in charge of the treasure convoy. As soon as he heard of the death of Nadir, and knowing the hatred in which the Persians held all Afghans, he at once fled the camp with his men and hastened to Kandahar. On arrival there he came upon the treasure convoy which was in charge of the rest of his contingent, and at once seized it.

With the wealth thus fortuitously acquired he bought over all the principal chiefs of both Afghanistan and Balochistan, and by their unanimous consent was crowned king at Kandahar, on an eminence overlooking the plain on which the present city stands. He immediately dismantled Nadirabad, and founded the modern city, which he named Ahmad Shahr, or Ahmad Shahi, and made his capital and royal residence. It is more generally known by the name of the original capital Kandahar, and is said to occupy the very spot on which the adventurous Afghan seized the treasure convoy—the accidental means of his elevation to royalty. It is a better town than the wretched production of Nadir, and stands on the high road across an open plain, about two miles to the north of it. At best it is but a poor collection of mud-built houses crowded together within fortified walls, and contains but a single building of any architectural merit—namely, the mausoleum of its founder himself.

AHMAD KHAN was crowned king in 1747 as Ahmad Shah, Durri Durrán, or "Pearl of Pearls," and the title is said to have been adopted from the distinctive custom of the Abdáli tribe of wearing a small pearl studded ring in the right ear.

In the following year he took Kabul from the Persian Governor, who had been left in it by Nadir, and thus established his authority in the home country. The rest of his prosperous reign of twenty-six years was occupied in an unceasing course of conquest and plunder. He repeatedly replenished his leaky coffers by successive invasions of India, raised the name of his nation to a high pitch of renown, opened a career for the ambition and greed of his hungry and luxurious nobles by foreign conquests, and, at his death, left an empire extending from the Sutlej and the Indus on the east to the Persian desert on the west; from the Oxus on the north to the Arabian sea on the south. He had gained as wife for Tymur, his son and heir-apparent, the daughter of the Dehli Emperor, and with her as dowry Lahore and all Panjab. Ahmad Shah's career was one of conquest and plunder throughout. Born and bred a soldier, he lived and died a soldier. He provided his restless and lawless people with congenial employment, and opened to his fickle and ambitious nobles rich fields for the gratification of their desires. But he did nothing for the substantial benefit of his country. His code of laws and regulations for the government of the home country was an ideal more than a real one. His people and country remained much the same as they were before, with the difference only that the wealth and pageantry of a newly-created court attracted many from a pastoral and wandering life to one of court etiquette and more settled habits. But as a whole, the people and country in their respective conditions were hardly affected by the new state of things. The one continued to be the lawless, restless, and ambitious people, greedy for wealth without the labour of honestly earning it, which they had always been noted to be—this last quality being a trait in the character of the nation which received a very powerful impetus by the enormous riches they acquired under the successful and repeated expeditions of their king. And the other remained undeveloped, without roads, and without security for the traveller.

AHMAD SHAH died in 1773, and was succeeded by the heir of his choice, his second son Tymur. The first act of the new king was to put down the opposition of his elder brother, Sulemán, by putting out his eyes. He then gave himself up to pleasure and the pageantry of court life, and left the government of the country to his ministers and provincial administrators. He changed the capital from Kandahar to Kabul, and generally spent the winter at Peshawar, which became a sort of second capital. The reign of Tymur was a complete contrast to that of his father. The repeated military expeditions and hauls of treasure, the restless activity and constant annexations of territory, which characterized the former, now gave way to luxury and pageantry at home, to minstrels and bayaderes, to pigeon-fancy and cock-fighting. Province after province of the conquered states cut adrift and fell away from the newly-raised empire. Finally the treasury, failing to be replenished as heretofore from abroad, ran dry; discontent became rife, and the first signs of the coming storm began to show themselves. Tymur personally was despised as an effeminate voluptuary, but he was tolerated as the son of his father; and this fact, more than any other, shows the high estimation in which Ahmad Shah was held by his people, for he is now hardly known except by name, the commotions and usurpations of succeeding years having fixed the minds of the people to more recent heroes, though of meaner calibre.

Indeed the events of the short decade of Nadir Shah's rule over this country are better known than those of the full quarter-century of the Durrani sovereigns' reign. The one was a conqueror who destroyed and subjugated, who planted Persian governors of a comparatively civilized stamp, and who ruled as an autocrat. The other was the leader of a banditti, who ravaged and plundered, and was subservient to the will of his supporters and followers. The deeds of the one are remembered—of the other forgotten.

TYMUR died in 1793, after a reign of twenty years, and left a score or so of sons, and a larger number of daughters. Of his sons, Zamán was governor of Kabul, Abbás of Peshawar, Kuhndil of Kashmir, Humáyún of Kandahar, and Mahmúd of Herat. And this was all that remained of the Durrani Empire of Ahmad Shah at the death of his successor. It was merely the native or Pukhtún country, with Kashmir added.

ZAMAN SHAH succeeded to the throne through the support of Payanda Khan, the prime minister of his father. This able and astute minister was the son of the celebrated Haji Jamál, Barakzai, who had been the most active partizan and supporter of Ahmad Shah when he was first made king; and his object in now taking Zamán in hand was to use him as a puppet whilst he matured his own ambitious designs. Zamán, however, had no sooner ascended the throne than his right was contested by Humáyún at Kandahar, and by Mahmúd at Herat. He immediately marched against Kandahar and reduced the former, and then proceeded to Herat, where he was forced to a compromise owing to rebellion at Kabul. In the midst of these troubles, Agha Muhammad Khan, the founder of the present Cájár dynasty, came to the throne of Persia, and, having seized Khurásán, demanded the cession of Balkh, which still nominally pertained to the Kabul Government. Zamán, unable to resist, ceded the province in the hope of making a friend of the Persian for the furtherance of his own ulterior designs on India; for it seems to have become clear to him that the Durrani Empire, founded on the plunder of India, could not be kept a-going without periodical supplies from that inexhaustible source. With the alienation of Balkh came the revolt of the Panjab, which was an appanage of the Empire as dower of Tymur's wife, and Zamán was content to appoint Ranjit Sing as his ruler at Lahore.

At this juncture Payanda Khan, the prime minister,

finding the moment opportune for dethroning the puppet whom he found less flexible than he had reckoned, entered into a league with Shujá-ul-Mulk (the brother of Zamán) to set him on the throne. The plot, however, was discovered to Zamán, who forthwith executed Payanda Khan and his fellow conspirators. On this Fath Khan, the son of Payanda, went over to the side of Mahmúd, and, with aid derived from Persia, seized upon Kandahar and installed Mahmúd there. Zamán, forsaken by his supporters, sent an army for the recovery of Kandahar, but it deserted to Mahmúd, who, thus strengthened, marched against Kabul, defeated and captured Zamán, and put out his eyes. The blind monarch ultimately proceeded to Ludhiana, and there became a pensioner of the British Government.

Having established himself at Kabul, Mahmúd next seized Peshawar from Shujá-ul-Mulk, who fled at his approach dreading the vengeance of Fath Khan. This occurred at the commencement of the present century, and was followed immediately by a rising of the Ghilzais to contest the government with Mahmúd. They were defeated by Fath Khan, but revolted again in the following year, and suffering a second defeat subsided into quiet. Meanwhile Mahmúd had returned to Kabul, and he had no sooner turned his back on Peshawar, than Shujá, collecting his supporters and a considerable force, marched against him, and in 1803—the year the East India Company took Dehli—captured Kabul and imprisoned Mahmúd. Whilst this was enacting at Kabul, the Cájár King of Persia made an attempt to seize on Herat, but his governor of Khurásán, who led the expedition, was defeated. Following this, the Government of India, apprehensive of the meditated invasion of India by Napoleon in co-operation with Alexander of Russia, decided on opening relations with Shah Shujá-ul-Mulk, and despatched Elphinstone's Mission to Peshawar, where the British envoy met the Durrani Sovereign and concluded a treaty. This occurred in 1809, and marks the first dealings of the British with the Afghans.

It is curious to note the difference in the opinion then formed of this people, and that which is now held of them after an acquaintance of just seventy years. The fine, hospitable, courteous, and chivalrous Afghan of that day, is to-day the proud, fickle, blustering, and treacherous intriguer in whom there is no faith, and to rely on whose word is to court disaster. Truly the latter—proved by dear-bought experience on more than one occasion—is not short of the mark.

Following this memorable transaction at Peshawar, Fath Khan, deserting his allegiance to Shujá and pursuing the ambition of his father, plotted the restoration of Mahmúd. He effected his escape from prison and junction with himself at Kandahar, and then, as Wazir, marched with his protegé against Kabul. Shujá was defeated and forced to fly the country, and, after many hardships and perilous adventures, finally joined his brother Zamán at Ludhiana, where he also became a pensioner of the Indian Government—of the East India Company.

With the re-establishment of Mahmúd at Kabul with Fath Khan as his prime minister, the affairs of the government underwent a remarkable change. The minister was king, and the king was a pampered debauchee. Fath Khan now had the game he had been playing for in his own hands. He knew the character of his people well, and took care to make himself popular with them by open-handed liberality and the forms of hospitality common to the country. Meanwhile he was not neglectful of his own interests, and the necessity of strengthening his position; and these ends he secured by distributing the most important of the local and provincial governments amongst his own sons and adherents. The popularity and power now acquired by Fath Khan did not escape the notice of Mahmúd, and he became jealous of his Wazir. The time, however, was not opportune for an open rupture with so powerful a servant, and the mistrustful king bided his time. The Persians had for some time been meddling and intriguing in the affairs of Herat, and, in 1816, had got possession of the place. Fath Khan was sent to clear them out, which, with his usual good fortune, he did very promptly and effectually. His success, however, only increased the enmity of Mahmúd, and roused the jealousy of his son Kamrán.

In 1818, on some trivial pretence, he was made a prisoner by Mahmúd and handed over to Kamrán, who, to prevent further chance of the more than suspected schemes of the Wazir growing to maturity, deprived him of sight by thrusting a red-hot pin into his eyes—an act of barbarity, which, it is said, the savage young prince committed with his own hands. On this, all the Barakzai chiefs—brothers and sons of Fath Khan—rose in revolt, and Mahmúd was driven from Kabul by Dost Muhammad Khan. The fugitive made a stand at Ghazni, but unable to resist the impetuosity of his pursuer, continued his flight to Herat; but, before doing so, Mahmúd and Kamrán vented their hatred of the helpless prisoner in their hands by putting him to death with the most horrible tortures. The murder of Fath Khan raised a storm of vengeance, which sealed the doom of the Saddozai, Fath Khan sacrificed his life in the game he played for, but it was not lost, his family took it up, and with the sympathy of the whole nation won it. The Barakzai came into power under Dost Muhammad, who, in 1826, established himself at Kabul, whilst his brother Sherdil held Kandahar.

And thus ended the Durrani Empire. It rose up by accident, and went down by misrule, after enduring just three score and ten years. The vigorous reign of its founder, Ahmad Shah, was a period of ambition, conquest, and plunder. The feeble reign of his successor was one of pleasure, paralysis, and decline. And the unstable reigns of the succeeding competitors, Zamán, Shujá, and Mahmúd, were a period of anarchy and discord, of treachery and torture, of convulsions and death. With such a career no empire could be expected to endure. The Afghan, who, with mushroom growth, rose into the position of the ruling race, possessed none of the qualities requisite to the situation. But recently reclaimed from a wild nomadic life, still illiterate and unpolished, he failed to attach to his interests the copartners in the soil, to conciliate his compatriots, and to secure their loyalty and support. He stood alone amid the various races which composed the nation over which he had acquired the dominion; and he fought out his quarrels amongst his own people. His relations with his neighbours were vicarious and unreliable, and he had neither the countenance nor the support of either the Paramount Power of the East or of that of the West.

And so it was that the Durrani Empire sunk and disappeared, but not so the Durrani rule. This merely passed from one family of the race to another—from the Saddozai to the Barakzai. With this transfer of rule, however, there came a complete change over the status of the country. The empire had passed away and was replaced by the principality. The Shah gave way to the Amir—the Emperor to the Prince. But besides this, there was a change of a more noteworthy and important character. The home kingdom which was all that remained of the empire, no longer continued an integral whole acknowledging the central authority at Kabul. On the contrary, it became split up into the independent chiefships of Herat under Kamrán—the last representative of the Saddozai family; Kandahar under Sherdil and his brothers joint partners in the government—Kuhndil and Rahmdil; and Kabul under Dost Muhammad. Peshawar still remained in the hands of Sultan Muhammad, but he held the place only as governor under Ranjit Sing, who, during the confusion following on the murder of Fath Khan, seized Kashmir in 1819 and this place four years later.

When Dost Muhammad took up the reins of government at Kabul—the recognized capital of the country—he assumed the leadership of the divided nation, and adopted the title of Amir—the first Amir of Afghanistan. The word is an Arabic one, and means "Commander." It was first introduced as a military title by the Khálifs under the form Amirul-Muminin, or "Commander of the Faithful," and was bestowed upon provincial governors who were subordinate to the Khiláfat, or Caliphate, as most Europeans write the word. Subsequently it became adopted as a princely title by independent rulers of the minor states which looked to the head of the Faith as their paramount power. And latterly it came to carry with it a sense of subordination in the ranks of sovereignty.

With the assumption of this title Dost Muhammad acquired nothing more than an acknowledged pre-eminence among the local chiefs of the country of which he held the capital. He acquired no extra power or territorial dominion with it, for, as a matter of fact, his authority was limited to Ghazni on one side of his capital, and Jalalabad on the other.

Whilst Afghanistan was being thus partitioned between the sons of Fath Khan, the course of affairs between Herat and Persia did not run smoothly; and in 1834 a Persian army under Abbas Mirza, the son and heir-apparent of Fath Ali Shah, the reigning Cájár Sovereign, marched against Herat, but was withdrawn on a compromise with the isolated Kamrán. About this time Shujá, the refugee at Ludhiana, seeing the dismembered and disorganized state of the country, set out with a large army to recover his lost kingdom, and marched against Kandahar. Here Kuhndil, holding out, summoned the aid of Dost Muhammad from Kabul, and on his arrival, Shujá, being defeated with the loss of most of his army, was forced to fly to Herat. His nephew Kamrán, however, closed the gates against him, and the disappointed Saddozai had to turn back and find his way across the Sístan desert to Calát or Kelát, where Nasír Khan gave him asylum, and sent him on to Ludhiana.

This victory at Kandahar established the authority of the Barakzai, whilst the conduct of Kamrán reduced the cause of the Saddozai to a hopeless condition, and raised the hopes of the Persian king in his ultimate views regarding Herat. While these events were enacting in Afghanistan, Fath Ali Shah was succeeded as king of Persia by his grandson Muhammad Shah. And he, instigated by General Simonich, the Russian Minister at Tehran, marched against Herat and laid siege to the fortress. It was gallantly defended by the garrison under the guidance and encouragement of Lieut. Eldred Pottinger, who happened to be there at the time. Meanwhile, on the other side of the country, Dost Muhammad sent an army against the Sikhs at Peshawar to recover the Indus provinces which they had taken from the Kabul Government with the consent of Shujá. The Afghan army defeated the Sikhs at Jamrúd near the mouth of the Khybar, but as Dost Muhammad suspected that his success might rouse the jealousy of the Government of Lord Auckland, he endeavoured to strengthen himself by communicating with the Government of Russia, without, at the same time, ceasing his correspondence with the Government of India.

These two important events—the Persian siege of Herat and the Afghan defeat of the Sikhs, both at opposite ends of the kingdom of the Durrani—caused the British Government some anxiety, and, in 1837, Sir Alexander Burnes was sent to Kabul as British Envoy to settle affairs between Dost Muhammad and Ranjit Sing. This was the first instance of a British Envoy being installed at Kabul. He had not been there long when there arrived, towards the close of the same year, a Russian agent named Vitcovich. He was a mysterious individual, and acted in a mysterious way. He travelled by Herat and Kandahar, and in the latter place made a treaty with the ruler, Kuhndil Khan, to defend Herat in the Persian interest. At Kabul he was so successful in his intrigues that he diverted the Amir from his contemplated alliance with the British, and, estranging Dost Muhammad from Burnes, persuaded him to break off negotiations with the British Envoy.

In the meantime, the siege of Herat, which had continued for three or four months without much success, was abandoned by the Persians in consequence of the action of the British fleet in the Persian Gulf, and, Dost Muhammad proving obdurate, the British Government took up the cause of Shujá-ul-Mulk, the refugee at Ludhiana, as the rightful sovereign of Afghanistan, and decided on restoring him to his usurped throne in the hope of his proving a loyal ally and effective buffer against the Persians and Russians. As a first step towards this proceeding, the famous Tripartite Treaty was concluded. Shujá, on his own part, made a treaty with Ranjit Sing, ceding to him all the Indus provinces which the Sikhs had taken from the Afghans; and Ranjit, on his part, agreed to assist the British advance on Kabul to set Shujá in the place of Dost Muhammad.

CHAPTER IV.

BRITISH RELATIONS WITH AFGHANISTAN.

In the first days of 1839, Shujá-ul-Mulk joined the army of the Indus under Sir John (afterwards Lord) Keane, and arriving at Kandahar, after a victorious march by the Bolan, was there crowned Shah, as rightful heir of the "Durrani Empire," on the 8th May, with great pomp and ceremony. In the following month, Shah Shujá-ul-Mulk marched from Kandahar towards Kabul with the British army, which on the way there took Ghazni for him after a short siege and brilliant assault. On the fall of Ghazni, Dost Muhammad fled beyond the Hindu Kush, and the British army advancing entered Kabul in August, and there set Shah Shujá on "the throne of his ancestors"—a first grandfather. With this brilliant exploit was secured the first triumph of the British policy. It was short lived, however, and ended in disaster. For a time all went smoothly, and British gold and justice were much appreciated by the people. But presently, owing to the indiscreet and unwarrantable interference of our "politicals," and their ignorance of the character of this independent people, so different in every particular from the meek and cringing native of Hindustan, a very marked change came over the aspect of affairs.

We had set up a king on "the throne of his ancestors" with every available pomp and parade, had declared him sovereign of the Durrani Empire, and then at once, through our politicals, denied him the exercise of his legitimate powers, and even thwarted his wishes in matters of the most trivial importance —errors of judgment, which, though lightly considered by us, were, nevertheless, unbearably galling to the sensitiveness and pride of an Eastern king.

After the enthronement of Shah Shujá, Dost Muhammad returned to Kabul from his asylum with the ruler of Khulm and tendered his submission to the British Envoy. He was sent off to India with some of his wives and two of his sons, and they became pensioners of the British Government. With the deportation of Dost Muhammad the most dangerous and only serious factor of hostility was removed, and the Shah naturally looked for the surrender of his kingly functions by the British Envoy, and was impatient for the departure of the British army. His wishes, however, did not suit the views of the British Government, although the expense of maintaining their troops, at so great a distance from their base, was become a question of serious perplexity. Added to this, the Shah was himself straitened for means to meet the charges on his own government. To obviate these difficulties, measures were set on foot to reduce the State pensions of the Sirdars or Barons—pensions which had been originally granted for military service to be rendered whenever the Shah took the field.

These measures, adopted with the object of reducing the expenses of the British occupation, very soon produced a very discontented feeling among the Barons, and they openly expressed their disloyalty and threats of hostility. The ferment among the nobles and chiefs thus created by these measures of 1840 went on increasing all through the following year, but were in a most extraordinary manner neglected by our highest officials, though it was at the time well known that the priesthood were unusually energetic in stirring up the people against us. In this state of the public mind, the Government reduced the allowances of the Ghilzai chiefs in the country between Kabul and Jalalabad. They were the tinder, the Shah the match, and the British Envoy struck the two together. The spark was caught up and immediately burst into flame, which spread as a great conflagration through all the Ghilzai tribes from Kandahar to Jalalabad. The Ghilzais were joined by the neighbouring hill-men and nomades, and the communications of the British army were cut off on all sides.

The march of Sale to Jalalabad from Kabul to open the road, and his gallant defence of that place, are matters of history and proud memorials. The subsequent course of events at Kabul, and the retreat of the British army, in January, 1842, on the plighted word of a sanguinary and notoriously faithless enemy, are also matters of history; but we would fain pass them by in silence, and cover them with the veil of mourning. On the departure of the British army from Kabul, dissensions arose in the court of the Shah, and he was murdered.

Then followed Pollock's avenging army. It reached Kabul in September of the same year, and was there joined by Nott's force from Kandahar. Our captives were recovered, punishment was inflicted on the city, and the avenged army set out on its march to India in the following month. The brilliant exploits of Nott and Pollock served as a salve to heal the wounded pride of the British nation, and the nation willingly accepted the vengeance exacted as wiping out the disgrace of our disastrous retreat. It was not so viewed by the Afghans however, who, careless of life themselves and accustomed to scenes of death and destruction, only remembered that a British army came to their country, retreated, and was annihilated on the march out. It is the memory of this success of theirs that has confirmed them in their haughty pride of national prowess, and in their belief in their superiority to us as a military people; whilst, further, it has increased their hatred of us as infidels and aggressive foreigners.

On the return of the British army to India, Dost Muhammad was released and forthwith repaired to Kabul, where he was at once received with open arms as Amir. Kuhndil at the same time returned to Kandahar from his asylum in Persia. Whilst Herat remained in the hands of Yar Muhammad, who had murdered Kamrán at the time the British army evacuated Kabul. And now all Afghanistan was in the hands of the Barakzai.

We need not follow the confused course of family jealousies and contests between Kabul, Kandahar, and Herat; nor need we stop to inquire into the reasons that induced Dost Muhammad to march to Attock in aid of the Sikhs against the British in the Panjab campaign. It will suffice for our purpose to state that Dost Muhammad, for the first eight years after his return to Kabul, was Amir only of that province from Ghazni to Jalalabad. He did not conquer Balkh till 1851—the first step in his scheme of a consolidated Afghanistan. Three years later, he made overtures for an alliance with the British Government, and these being well responded to, in January, 1855, he sent his son and heir-apparent, Ghulam Hydar Khan, to Peshawar, and a treaty of friendship was concluded there through the Commissioner of the Panjab, Sir John Lawrence. In August of the same year, Kuhndil died at Kandahar, and the Amir, three months later, took the place and annexed it to his dominions. This second step gained, he was now anxious to secure Herat also, which was threatened by Persia, but before he had time to arrange matters, the Persians took possession of the place. On this Dost Muhammad appealed to the British Government for aid to recover this important frontier of his kingdom, and following this up came to Peshawar, and there, in the beginning of 1857, concluded a treaty with Sir John Lawrence. Shortly after his departure, war was declared against Persia, and Lumsden's mission was sent to Kandahar, where it remained for fourteen months at the court of the heir-apparent, Hydar Khan.

After the evacuation of Herat by the Persians, the place was made over to Sultan Khan, Barakzai, who was an enemy of the Amir, and notoriously a protegé of the Shah. In 1858 he received and hospitally entertained the Russian exploring expedition under M. Khanikoff. The Amir, disappointed in his hopes of Herat, turned his attention in another direction, and, in 1859, annexed Kunduz, and secured the submission of Badakshan, a third step towards the consolidation of his kingdom. Herat only remained to complete it, and this place he took in 1863 after a siege of ten months. The Amir, by this last victory of his long, and active, and adventurous life, attained the desire of his heart, a consolidated Afghanistan. For his success he was indebted entirely to the alliance and support of the British Government. But this fact did not in in any way draw closer the relations between the two States.

On the contrary, the Amir never ceased his vigilance in closing his country against the European; and whilst pleading the hostility of his people against the race, lost no opportunity of abusing them himself, and openly encouraged his fanatic priesthood in vilifying them. His repeated, and almost dying, injunction to his heir-apparent, Sher Ali, was to keep on good terms with the British and hold fast by their alliance, but on no account, as he valued his throne, to let an Englishman set foot in the country.

Dost Muhammad was not destined to enjoy the fruits of his success at Herat. He died there on the 9th June, 1863, only a few days after the place fell into his hands. His son, Sher Ali, whom he had nominated heir-apparent, against the advice of his nobles and most loyal adherents, succeeded as Amir. He had, it is true, a consolidated kingdom ready to hand, but with it was to come the storm that had been predicted on all sides for years past. Perhaps it is well it was so, for Sher Ali had no taste for the tame life of home government, and could not have resisted the bent of his desire for foreign conquest had he not been more seriously engaged at home.

He was never a popular man. As a child he was wayward and quarrelsome. As a youth he was under the restraint of captivity in India, but his selfish and whimsy temper prevented his deriving any benefit from the cultivated society he was there brought into relations with. As a man in his capacity of Governor of Ghazni, he acquired an evil reputation; his rule was hard, and his punishments were spiteful and cruel; whilst his temper was such that it was sometimes thought he was wrong in the head. He had fits of vice and piety alternately, with intervals in which his best friends dreaded to meet the whims of his temper. For weeks together he would be shut up in his Harem with drugs and wines, and then for weeks he would be employed with the priests performing prayers, reading the Kuran, and listening to theological dissertations. He hated the English, and did not conceal the fact even when outwardly on the most friendly terms with them; and when the British were in the midst of their troubles with the mutiny in India, he was the most violent advocate in the old Amir's durbar for an attack upon them at Peshawar. Such was Sher Ali at the time he succeeded his father as Amir, not of Kabul, but of Afghanistan.

CHAPTER V.

SHER ALI.

Sher Ali, having performed the funeral rites of his father at Herat, left the place in charge of his son Yacúb, and set out for Kabul. On the march commenced the entangled chain of intrigues, plots, and disaffections which were soon to throw the country into civil war. Sher Ali reached Kabul in September, and passed the winter there undisturbed. In spring began the looked-for hostilities. His elder brothers, Afzal, Governor of Balkh, and Azim of Kurram, were the first to oppose him. He at once sent a force against the latter, who was defeated, and fled into British territory where he found asylum at Rawal Pindi. Against the former the Amir marched in person. He inveigled Afzal into his camp on fair promises, and then made him prisoner. After securing Balkh and settling the affairs of the country, Sher Ali returned to Kabul. He was now opposed by Amín Khan, his own brother, at Kandahar. He took the field against him, and on 6th June, 1865, fought the battle of Kajbaz near Kelat-i-Ghilzai, in which, though he won the victory, he lost both his brother and his son and heir elect, Muhammad Ali—nephew and uncle having fallen together in single combat. Sher Ali went on to Kandahar, and immediately gave himself up to grief for the double bereavement; and it was a grief peculiar to the man's temperament and characteristic thereof. He shut himself up for several months, during which time he continued in a despondent, morose, and irritable state of mind, and was at one time supposed to have lost his reason.

Whilst Sher Ali was thus inactive at Kandahar, Abdurrahman, son of the imprisoned Afzal, seized Balkh, and pushing forward took Kabul in February, 1866. The news of this loss suddenly roused Sher Ali from his lethargy, and he set out for Kabul without delay, with Afzal prisoner in his camp. Abdurrahman advanced to meet him, and the two armies came into action near Shekhabad, on the Ghazni road, on the 10th May, when Sher Ali was defeated and put to flight. Afzal was now released, and being joined by his brother Azim, proceeded with his son to Kabul, where he was well received, and at once proclaimed Amir.

Sher Ali, after some stay at Kandahar, proceeded to Herat in the beginning of February, 1867, and thence he joined Fyz Muhammad, who had come over to his side, in Turkestan. It was at this time that Sher Ali sent his son Yacúb, Governor of Herat, to meet the Shah of Persia at Mashhad. Whatever the nature of the interview, Sher Ali and Fyz Muhammad presently advanced towards Kabul. Abdurrahman went out to Hindu Kush to oppose them, and in the fight that ensued Fyz Muhammad was killed and Sher Ali put to flight. He stayed for some time in Balkh, and then returned to Herat, where he arrived in January, 1868. Meanwhile, the ruling Amir, Afzal, died at Kabul in October preceding, and was succeeded as Amir by Azim.

The rule of both these temporary Amirs had proved very unpopular, owing partly to their licentious habits and oppressive rule, and partly to the strong measures they adopted to procure the means for carrying on the war. The moment seemed opportune for Sher Ali to essay another attempt to recover his capital. In April, 1868, he sent forward Yacúb to take Kandahar, which was held by Sarwar, the son of Azim. This he did without much opposition, and was joined there by his father in the following June. Some time was spent here in preparations and buying over Azim's troops, and then in September, Sher Ali, Yacúb leading the way, recovered

Kabul, avoiding Azim, who had come out to oppose him at Ghazni, by a detour through Zurmat. On this Azim's troops went over bodily to Sher Ali; and he himself fled to Turkistan. Here he managed to raise a fresh force and made an attempt to re-take Kabul, in January of the following year. He was signally defeated and forced to flee with only a few attendants to Persia, where he died some months later.

SHER ALI, having now re-established himself as Amir on the throne of Kabul, at once threw himself on the protection of the British Government, and came to India to meet the Viceroy, Lord Mayo, at Amballa. The reception accorded him was most honorable and splendid, and Sher Ali went back to Kabul highly flattered and pleased with everything except the real business he had come upon. Apart from this disappointment, the Amir had very good reason to be amply satisfied and deeply grateful—if indeed there be such a quality as gratitude in the Afghan nature. He had received a reception which was not only flattering to himself, but was an honor conferred on his nation; he was acknowledged before all the world as the Amir of Kabul and the friend of the British Government. The consequence was that the consolidated Afghanistan which he inherited from his father and which he had lost during five years of civil war, came back to his hands in its integrity; and there was not a man in the country bold enough to raise a finger against the ally of the British.

For the first three years the renewed relations of the two Governments proceeded smoothly enough, and with high promise for the future. The success of the policy initiated by Lord Mayo was proved by the fruit it bore. The former professed enemy of the British seemed to have changed his dislike, and was lavish in his professions of devotion and attachment, and equally lavish in his expectations of further favours. The province of Badakhshan and the northern boundary of Afghanistan were secured for the Amir by the

British Government after long negotiation with the Russian Government. Sistan remained a question in dispute between the Amir and the Shah of Persia. Its settlement was submitted by the contending parties to the arbitration of the British Government. Their decision was given against the Amir, and it was more than he could bear. It undid all the good effected by the Amballa interview; and the newly-made friend reverted to the professed enemy of old.

The growing confidence and freer communications which were the first results of the salutary influence effected by Lord Mayo's most successful treatment of the fickle Afghan, were at once nipped in the bud, and replaced by a sulky reserve which it was impossible to remove by any reasonable amount of conciliation or forbearance. Russian advances and intrigues, which Sher Ali had, since his return to Kabul from the Amballa interview, either rejected or played with at arm's length, were now courted and entered into with a freedom which was incompatible with his friendship with both parties, and directly menacing to that with the British.

At the time of Dost Muhammad's death the Afghan regular army was less than thirty thousand infantry, with perhaps a hundred guns and six or eight thousand cavalry. At the close of his reign, Sher Ali's army was more than sixty thousand disciplined infantry, with fully three hundred guns, and perhaps sixteen thousand cavalry. It was a force five times greater than was needed for the home requirements of the country, and double the strength that the revenues of the country could support.

With this force at his command, Sher Ali felt himself strong, and fancied he could treat the great British Government, which had made him the Amir he was, with the indifference he might show to a petty state. Nay more, as his communications and relations with Russia increased and became more intimate, rumours floated about of a demand of a cession to the Kabul Government of the former Afghan possessions in India, which were now held by the British Government and formed part of the Indian Empire—down to Jhelam some reports said, and others down to Lahore itself.

The forbearance of the British Government, and their most earnest efforts to come to a satisfactory understanding with the Amir, were treated by Sher Ali with studied indifference and insulting delay; whilst access to his country from the side of India was rigidly closed to all but his own subjects, who came and went as if the two States were on the best of terms. Meanwhile, Russia, being encouraged, was no way backward in responding with big promises and alluring pictures of the future. And the proud and ignorant Sher Ali, after refusing to receive an English envoy at his court, filled the measure of his offences against the British Government by receiving a Russian mission at Kabul, entertaining them with marked honors and hospitality, and introducing them in public *darbár* to the principal nobles of the nation, summoned for the purpose from all parts of the kingdom.

Even this did not at once turn the tables of British forbearance. Yet another opportunity and time for reflection were to be allowed the obdurate Amir, and he was asked to receive a British Mission. The request was rejected in a very insulting manner, and then went forth the order for the British troops to invade Afghanistan. The Amir's forces at the Khybar and Pewar Passes were defeated with the loss of all their artillery and camps; and Sher Ali, with his Russian guests, quitting the capital, hurried across the Hindu Kush. Kabul, which the fugitive Amir had left in charge of Yacúb, whom he had just liberated from prison, was at our mercy; but we did not exercise that mercy. Instead of being so merciful as to march to Kabul, as we had done to Kandahar we were content to stop midway, not only in our road, but in our work as well. The Afghan, who was thoroughly cowed by the rapidity and brilliant character of the exploits of our armies at Kandahar, Pewar, and the Khybar, now plucked up courage in the very natural—however false it were—idea that we were afraid of him after all.

YACUB KHAN came down to the British camp at Gandumak to be acknowledged as Amir, and make a treaty of peace, with this idea of our timidity uppermost in his mind. His whole conduct whilst there proves that he did not consider himself or his country in our power. He saw us eager for a peace and a treaty. He on his part was eager to get us out of his country and take up the rôle which his father, who died in his refuge at Mazari Sharif beyond the Hindu Kush whilst these operations were in course of prosecution, had left him to carry to completion. To him a treaty with the British, whilst the relations of the Kabul Government with Russia were still unbroken, was not the serious thing he should have understood it to be. He had never been a friend of the British, his tendencies were on the other side. Though an intriguer, and ambitious from his youth up, he had never evinced any partiality for the British alliance. And it was his hostility against his father, after the Amir's return from Amballa, that drove Sher Ali to make a close prisoner of him. It was out of prison that he came to Gandumak to sign a treaty with a subordinate British officer, and to get rid of us. He accepted our articles, even to the forgiving of his enemies, and to the reception in his capital of a British Embassy; but he had no intention to carry them out. And this, as was at the time predicted, and in many instances openly stated by those of his sirdars in our interest, has now been proved, sadly to our cost—by the massacre in one day of our Envoy, his staff, and escort, to the number of one hundred and twenty-three souls—all within a stone's throw of his own palace, without the Amir so much as moving a finger to help his overwhelmed guests, fighting as they were for their lives like heroes of the Homeric period.

YACUB KHAN, on the 26th May, 1879, signed the Gandumak Treaty. On the 24th July he received the British Envoy, and installed him in the embassy assigned for his residence in the Bala Hissar of the city. On the 3rd September they were all destroyed by two regiments of his own household troops supposed to be in open mutiny, though they furnished guards around the Amir's palace at the very time that their comrades were doing to death a handful of strangers, the confiding guests of their master. Yacub, after the dastardly tragedy had been enacted, punished not a soul. His thoughts were turned to the subject of British vengeance, and, with strange ignorance, he satisfied himself that no British army would come to Kabul at least till the winter were past, during which interval there would be ample time to make arrangements to oppose it. How far he was out of his reckoning he has now learned very practically.

Within one month of the receipt of the particulars of the appalling fate of our Envoy and his party, a British army was before the walls of Kabul, and the Amir secure in its camp.

Such is the history, in briefest terms, of the Durrani Empire, and of the Durrani Principality to which it sunk in an ordinary lifetime. It is instructive, and affords food for reflection. And the question suggests itself why, after such a course of proved incapacity and faithlessness, should the Afghan be permitted to misrule any longer? or, why should he be permitted to hold the dominion and rule over better races of his compatriots! He is certainly not worthy of being entrusted with independent rule, and is as certainly not likely to submit to control until he has first been subjugated. Subjugation then is what is required for the Afghan. With him subjugated, all the races of the country will be easily controlled and governed. His subjugation is now to us a matter of no difficulty, and can be effected by placing in positions of command and rule men of other races.

It is the Afghan governors, from the Amir in his darbar to the meanest of his employés in the village police, who have diligently stirred up the animosity of the people against us, and excited their hatred by habitually abusing us. It has been the custom of each of the successive Amirs to vilify our name in public darbar and to encourage their courtiers in the same course. And any one who refrained from joining in this indiscriminate mode of expressing hostility was at once a marked man, and treated to the cold shoulder, with taunts of being an infidel at heart—a friend of the Farangi.

Yet the Amirs, whilst adopting this course of covert hostility as the rule of their conduct at home, had no hesitation in making treaties with us, in accepting subsidies from us, in strengthening their position by our too easily granted aid and support. In a word they had no hesitation in maintaining their position as the dominant race through our aid and countenance by a studied deception. Deception has all along been the guide of their conduct. Their constant references and appeals to the hatred and hostility which their people entertained against us was a mere excuse incriminating themselves, and proving their own double-facedness. With their hollow and self-interested professions of friendship and loyalty of alliance with us they have never once given us any tangible proof of the sincerity of their words. In so simple a matter of justice as the extradition, or even punishment at home, of a murderer, who, excited by their own evil example and the publicly-encouraged hostility of their priests, has come across the border in a fit of fanaticism and killed some unoffending European, they have never rendered us any justice. Our Government has tamely submitted to the indignity, and the Amirs have thus been encouraged in their course. The people take the cue from their leaders and rulers, and it is these who are really responsible for the worked-up hostility of the people. It is the Amirs, Sardars, and Khans who require to be subjugated by reduction from the position of dominance they hold, by exclusion from office in the administration of the country—a measure which there is no necessity to carry out at a swoop, but one which can be worked out gradually to the lasting advantage and salvation of the country.

The Afghans as a race certainly do hate us, mainly because from infancy they have been taught to do so. But they are not all so minded. There are many whom self-interest and acquaintance with us have taught to respect us, and if not to like us, to be at least friendly disposed towards us.

We have judged the Afghan as we have found him; and we have found him very wanting. He has his virtues and he has his vices, and to our mind the latter overbalance the former very heavily. He is not fit to govern either himself or others, and sadly wants a master. If we don't take up that rôle, Russia will. For a master the Afghans want, and a master they must have sooner or later. Which is it to be?

CHAPTER VI.

THE PATHAN.

THIS term has a very wide application as used by the people of India, and a very restricted one as used by the Patháns themselves. In the former case it is applied indiscriminately to all the peoples inhabiting the country now known as Afghanistan, including even the Tajík and Hazarah, who are both Persian-speaking people. In the latter case it is applied to Pukhto-speaking people only, and even then with a distinction, as the proper patronymic of certain tribes who are neither Afghan nor Ghilzai, but simply Pathán or Pukhtún. In this latter case it is the name applied to, and accepted by, the different peoples or races who speak the Pukhto language and inhabit the Pathán or Pukhtún country—much in the same way as a native of England, taken in the comprehensive sense of the word, is called Englishman, and accepts the name, whether he be in reality Irish, or Scotch, or Welsh;—that is to say, the Afghan and the Ghilzai are both Patháns, but the true Pathán is neither one nor the other, just as the Irish, Scotch, and Welsh are Englishmen, whilst the true Englishman is neither one nor the other of the three.

The origin of the term Pathán, and of the nationalities originally represented by it, carry us back to very early times. The term Pathán is not a native word at all. It is the Hindustani form of the native word Pukhtána, which is the plural of Pukhtún, or Pakhtún (the *a* as in our *pack*) as it is pronounced by the Afrídí. And Pukhtún is the proper patronymic of the people inhabiting the country called Pukhtún-khwá, and speaking the language called Pukhtú or Pukhto. What the meaning of the word Pukhta, from which Pukhtún and its above derivatives are held to come, may be is a matter of speculation. By some it is supposed to be the same word as the native *Pukhta*—a "ridge" or "hill"—in distinction to *Ghar*—a "mountain chain" or "peak,"—the two words corresponding respectively to the Persian *pushta* and *koh*. Be this as it may, and there is no denying the fact that the name Pukhtún-khwá—the "Pukhtún coast or quarter"—is very well in accordance with the character of the country in its physical aspect; there is also the fact that, in the time of Herodotus, four centuries before our era, this very country was called Pactiya or Pactiyica, and its natives Pactiyans. In Western Afghanistan, the harsh *kh* is changed into the soft *sh*, and Pukhtún becomes Pushtún, Pukhtú becomes Pushtú, and so on. By some Pukhtún tribes—the Afrídí notably—Pukhtún, Pukhtú, &c., are pronounced Pakhtún, Pakhtú, &c., and this brings the words nearer to the *Pakhtues* of Herodotus. In short, the Pakhtún or Pukhtún of to-day, we may take it, is identical in race and position with the Pactiyan of the Greek historian.

There is a very remarkable coincidence in terms, if nothing more, derivable from this word Pactiya. Herodotus mentions another and entirely distinct country of this name in the province of Armenia. And it is not difficult to trace the same name through the countries of Southern Europe to the ancient Pictavium—or modern Poictiers—in France, and thence on to the Picts of our own Islands. In fact, to the curious speculator in archæology, there is a wide field for enquiry and research in this Pakhtún-khwá country, where the Pacts and Scyths who inhabit it may be held to correspond with the Picts and Scots of our own country, whilst the Kambari of the Khan of Kelat's family, and large sections of the Afrídí people, called Kambar-khel and Kamari, together with the Logari of Logar or Lohgar, may be compared with the Cambrians and Logrians, of ancient Britain. Whether there be any connection or not between these names, their similarity and juxtaposition in such widely separated regions is at least noteworthy, if not deserving of more serious attention and investigation.

This Pactiya of Herodotus was a country bordering on the Indus, and the most eastern province of those into which the Empire of Darius Hystaspes was divided. It contained four contiguous nations, who were placed under the command of a single Satrap or Governor, and it corresponded in extent very nearly exactly with the modern Pukhtún-khwá, or "Pukhtún quarter." The term Pukhtún-khwá is a purely home word, and seldom heard from the mouth of a stranger. By outsiders and foreigners—on the side of India almost exclusively—the country is known by the name of Roh, which has the same signification as Koh—"mountain"— and its natives are called Rohilla—"mountaineer;" or Highlands, and Highlanders.

The four nations who dwelt in this country in the time of Herodotus were the Gandarii, the Aparytæ, the Sattagyddæ, and the Dadicæ. The first have long since been identified with the ancient inhabitants of that part of the Peshawar valley now known as the Yúsufzai and Mahmand country. The second and third (see Rawlinson's Herodotus) have hitherto been entirely unknown, and are now for the first time identified with the Afrídi, and the Khattak of the present day. The last, or Dadicæ, are still the subject of speculation, but are, I think, most probably represented by the nearly extinct tribe of the Dadi, who dwell amongst the Kakar, on the southern border of the ancient Sattagyddæ country. It is curious to find these very nations now, after a lapse of more than two thousand years, retaining the identical names and the same positions as those assigned to them by the ancient Greek author, who is justly styled the "Father of History."

To understand the relative positions of these four Pactiyan

nations, it will be as well first to take a glance at the ancient geography of the country, which in early times was known as Ariya Vartha to the Persians, and Ariana to the Greeks, afterwards as Khurásán, and in recent times only as Afghanistan. Its principal divisions, as brought to our knowledge by the Greeks, were, in ancient times, Bactria and Margiana on the north, Ariya and Zarangia or Drangia on the west, Paropamisus and Arachosia in the middle tract, and Pactiya and part of Bactria on the east with Gedrosid to the south. The limits of none of these are now accurately definable, though for practical purposes, their general position and extent are sufficiently well known.

BACTRIA—the Bakhtar of the Persians, the Bahlika of the Hindus, and Bactria of the Greeks may be considered to comprise all the country between the Upper Oxus or Wakhsh, as far west as the Balkh frontier, and the Upper Indus to the point where it is struck by the Dumah range running due east and west from the head waters of the Swat and Panjkora rivers—the Suastus and Guræas respectively of the Greeks. In a south-westerly direction, its border probably ran along the Bamian hills to Gardan Diwár, and thence along the Pughmán range to that of Altamúr—bounding the Logar and Wardak country to the southward—which connects the Sherdahán, or "Lion's Mouth" pass of Ghazni with the Pari-darra, or "Fairy Glen" of Jagdalak (not an inappropriate name with its ruby mines and gold diggings, though a spot of mournful memory as the scene of the greatest slaughter and climax of disasters that befel our retreating army in January, 1842); whilst onwards from this point the Kabul river, down to the junction with it of the Kunar or Chitrál stream, formed the boundary. In the north-east, the country which appears on our maps as Bolor, but in native books is written Balúr, was probably included in Bactria, and comprised the districts of Chitral or Káshkár, Yasín, Gilgit, and Skardo. In fact, it appears that the word

Balúr itself is merely a natural variant form of Bakhtar, as in the corresponding changes from the Persian *dukhtar* to the Pukhtú *lúr*, "daughter;" from *sokhtan* to *swal*, "to burn;" from *padandar* to *plandar*, "stepfather;" from *mádar* to *mor*, "mother;" from *padar* to *plár*, "father," and so on.

PACTIYA—the Pukhtún-khwá of the natives, and Roh of Muhammadan writers—apparently comprised all the country of the modern Sulemán range and the Sufed Koh, extending northward in one direction to the head waters of the Swat and Panjkora streams and the Dumah range, and in the other to the south banks of the Logar and Kabul rivers down to Jalalábád. The southern limit was, probably, the same as that of the present Kakar country, where it marches with the Peshín and Shál districts, and the Bori valley to the Indus. The eastern limit was the Indus itself. And the western, the Helmand, including thus the country of Arachosia of the Greeks—the Ar-Rúkháj of Arabian geographers, and the Zabul of the Muhammadan historians—to the south of Ghazni. And these, roughly stated, are the limits of the present Pukhtún-khwá. This territory was originally the seat of the true Pukhtún people, who were, as they still are, Indians—the Afghan, Ghilzai, Wazírí, Kakar, &c., &c., being later and comparatively modern immigrants and conquerors. Within these limits of the ancient Pactiya were located the four contiguous nations above-mentioned, who were, in the time of Darius, combined in a single satrapy, under a single satrap, but under military commanders of their own. Let us now proceed to consider each of these nations separately.

THE GANDARIANS—the Gandhárí of the natives, the Gandarii, or, including kindred tribes, the Gandaridæ of the Greeks—formerly occupied the tract of country enclosed between the Kabul and Indus rivers from the point of junction of the Kunar stream with the former, up to Chaghán Sarae and the Dumah range. In this extensive area are comprised the districts of Goshta, Bajawar, Swát, Buner, Chamla, Mahában, Yúsufzai or Mandar, Hastnaghar, Dáudzai, and Gandhár. In other words, the Gandaria of the Greeks and the Sindhú Gandhárá of the Indians, in the widest sense of the terms, comprised the Peshawar valley north of the Kabul river and the hills circling it in that direction up to the limits defined. In a more restricted sense, it was, it would appear limited to the tract between the junction angle of the Kabul and Swat rivers, bounded northward by the Kohi Mor mountain, and westward by the Kunar river. This tract includes the modern districts of Goshta, Gandhár, and Dáudzai, and may be taken to represent the Gandaritis of the Greeks.

It has been stated in a previous passage that, in the fifth or sixth century of our era, consequent to a very powerful irruption of various Scythic hordes from the northward, there took place an emigration *en masse* of the natives of Gandaria or Gandhárá, and that, on quitting their homes on the Indus, they journeyed westward and joined a kindred people amongst whom they established themselves as a powerful colony on the banks of the Helmand, and there, it would seem, founded a city, which they named Gandhár after their native capital—a name which survives in the name of the modern city and province of Kandahar.

At that time these people were known as Gandarians, or Gandhári. They were Budhists by religion, and carried with them in their long and arduous journey the most sacred relic of their religion left them—the water-pot of Budha—as has before been mentioned. What was their subsequent history in their new Gandhár, and whom they warred with and conquered, remains very much of a mystery, beyond the fact that they were Indians of a kindred race. It would seem clear, however, that for nigh two centuries they maintained their independence and their religion in all the country from the head waters of the Arghasan and Tarnak rivers in the east to the lower course of the Helmand through Garmsel to the borders of the Sistán lake and Farrah in the west;

from the valleys of Shál and Peshin or Foshang on the south, to those of the Arghandáb and Helmand on the north.

That they were not the only people inhabiting the country we learn from the accounts of the early Arab historians, who tell of a complex mixture of races, languages, customs, and religions so late as the first century of the Muhammadan era—the seventh-eighth of our own. It would seem, however, that they were decidedly the most powerful, and the dominant, of the several races who occupied the country with them. Among these latter we can certainly count the original Persian possessor, at that time of the Zoroastrian religion—a fire-worshipper. The Saka, too, who gave their name to the country of Sistán, were also long prior arrivals, as well as were the Tymanni and, perhaps, some Baloch tribes.

But whatever the composition of the population of the Kandahar country at that period, and it certainly contained no small element of Indian tribes—colonists during the Pándú rule at Ghazni and Kabul, long anterior to the Gandarian emigration—we are mainly interested here in tracing the fortunes and fare of the latter people. As before stated, their early history in the new settlements about the Helmand is involved in mystery. It seems probable, however, that they early succumbed to the force of Islám, and that the bond of religious brotherhood, characteristic of that creed, though slow in being put on, when once securely fastened, soon destroyed their national identity, except in the remains of patronymics and local names which serve to guide the enquirer more correctly than half-forgotten or falsified traditions.

It is probable that the Afghan people (who were neighbours of these Gandarians and had very early accepted Islám) took a very leading part, with the Arab conquerors, in the subjugation of the infidel inhabitants of Southern Afghanistan, and in their conversion to the Muhammadan creed. And, further, it is probable that, being the dominant race, they not only gave their own national name to their subjects, but, to a considerable extent, blended with them by intermarriage and the adoption of their language and many of their customs. And this, much in the same way as is in our day occurring under the dominance of the Durrani as an independent government; for, in a loose way, all the different peoples inhabiting Afghanistan call themselves Afghans by nationality, and are generally so considered by foreigners, much in the same way as the originally different peoples of England Proper now call themselves Englishmen.

How long it took for these western Gandarians to lose their own national name and identity, and to become incorporated in the Afghan people, is quite uncertain; but it would appear that about three or four hundred years ago, when the Afghan genealogies of the present day began to be concocted, they were already thoroughly mixed up with their conquerors, counted as of kindred race, and reckoned very good Musalmáns; which is more than can be said of the Patháu Proper, or of the Ghilzai.

It was in the first half of the fifteenth century, during the reign at Kabul of Mirza Ulugh Beg—the grandson of Tymur, or Tamerlane—that the retrograde emigration, previously mentioned, took place; when a large body of the Budhist Indians, converted to Islám, and the Gandarians, transformed into Afghans, returned to their native seat upon the Indus. The tribal traditions are to the effect that, about three or four hundred years ago, the Yúsufzai, or Mandar, and Mahmand tribes of Afghans were settled on the Ghwara Margha and the head waters of the Tarnak and Arghasan rivers as neighbours and allies. Beyond them, lower down the course of these rivers, were the Tarin, another tribe of Afghans, who still occupy the same positions, and the valley of Peshin. Their lands were in the summer subject to droughts, and were besides in great part waste, owing to the exhaustion at that season of the tributary streams and the diminished volume of the rivers. The consequence was a contest for the better lands, and the Tarin tribes, being the stronger of the two parties, gradually encroached upon the "Fat Pastures" (*Ghwara Margha*) of the Mandar and Mahmand tribes, and finally dispossessed them of their lands.

The ousted tribes then moved away bodily together with their cattle and flocks and tents, for at that time they were almost entirely nomadic in their mode of life. What induced them to make direct for the Peshawar valley—the ancient Gandhár—is a subject for enquiry. Whether they were guided by mere chance, or whether some tradition still lingered in the memory of their "Grey beards" that the country towards which they had set their faces with kith and kin, bag and baggage, was their true fatherland, is uncertain, though the latter would seem highly probable. It may be stated in this connection, that in native books on this subject the Yúsufzai, or Mandar, and Mahmand are merely mentioned by their tribal names, whilst the Tarin are specified as Afghans, indicating, as it were, some original distinction of race. Be this as it may, it is certain that, after quitting their lands in the west, the ousted tribes marched by Ghazni and Kabul to Nangrahár, and thence into the Peshawar valley.

In Nangrahár—the old name of the present Jalalábád valley (a name still commonly in use and supposed to signify "the nine rivers," though there is not that number in it, and explained to be a combination of the Persian *nuh* — "nine" and the Arabic *nahar* — "river," but which is in reality a word of much more ancient date and purely of Sanscrit derivation, Nau Vihárá, "the nine monasteries;" the valley having been a very flourishing seat of Budhism even so late as the time of Fa Hian's visit in the fifth century of our own era, and still abounding in topes and the ruins of other Budhist buildings) —the two tribes appear to have rested a while, and then to have advanced by separate routes. The Yúsufzai, or Mandar, and Mali, as the two great divisions of the tribe are named, proceeded by the Khybar route to Peshawar, which at that time was called Purshor (after Porus, the Indian king, who opposed Alexander the Great), and encamped about the site of Bagram (the name of an ancient city the ruins of which extend over a large area to the west of the present city of Peshawar, and contain several topes and other Budhist relics, some of which are covered by the British cantonment at this place), between the present city of Peshawar and the Khybar pass.

Their approach and arrival do not appear to have been opposed by the people of the country, and for a while they pastured their flocks on the wide waste at the mouth of the Khybar. Soon, however, disputes arose as to the use of the watercourses drawn from the Bara river for irrigation purposes, and fierce conflicts ensued between the Afghans and the possessors of the land, whom the Yúsufzai accounts describe as "infidels" of the Dalazak and other tribes, though the former had been nominally Musalmáns since their forcible conversion in the eleventh century by Mahmud of Ghazni; whilst the latter certainly included their own kindred of the parent stock, now known by the name of Hindki, a people who prior to the Muhammadan conquest extended as far west as Kabul, near which city a village of that name is a relic of their former presence.

Very little is known regarding the origin of the Dalazak people. There are grounds, however, for believing that they were originally of Scythic origin, and came into their position here with the great irruption of the Jat and Katti, which in the fifth or sixth century drove the native Gandarians to emigrate westward to the Helmand valley. This view is supported by the fact of their holding, at the time we are now speaking of, the Peshawar valley in conjunction with the kindred Jat people, whose representatives are still found there in considerable communities, scattered about in different villages under the name of Gujar, whose characteristic occupations are the rearing of cattle and the cultivation of the soil; and also by the fact that, on their expulsion across the Indus they, in considerable bodies, found shelter with the Jat peasantry of the Panjab, amongst whom the Gujar element is indicated by their settlements at Gujranwala, Gujrat, Gujarkhan, &c.

The Dalazak themselves were professedly Musalmáns, and had been so since the time of Mahmúd of Ghazni, who took a strong contingent of their troops with him to Somnath. They invaded Peshawar, it seems, in great force through the Khybar, and very rapidly possessed themselves of the whole valley to the Indus and the foot of the northern hills, reducing the natives to subjection, or driving them into the mountain retreats of Buner, Swat, and Bajawar. They were an important and powerful people here, till defeated and driven across the Indus by the Yúsufzai and Mahmand in the time of Mirza Ulugh Beg.

CHAPTER VII.

THE YUSUFZAI.

The Yúsufzai, after six years of constant warfare, drove the Dalazak across the Indus into Chach and Paklí, and thus acquired full possession of the plain country which now bears their name, and lies between the Swat *cum* Kabul rivers. During another succeeding period of fourteen years of constant warfare with their "infidel" kindred (called Gandhárí and Hindki) and the Gujar settlers, the Yúsufzai pushed their conquest into the hills on the north and north-west as far as the sources of the Panjkora and Swat rivers, and the country drained by the Barandú, which is a direct tributary of the Indus.

In this twenty years' war the Yúsufzais exterminated some small sections of the natives, drove others across the Indus into Chach and Paklí in one direction, and across the Kunar river into Chitral and Katár (the present Kafiristan) in the other, and subjugating the greater number to serfdom, converted them to the Muhammadan creed, and called them Hindki in distinction to the idolatrous Hindú. These Hindki were in all probability the representatives of the remnant of the native Gandhárí, who were subjugated by their Jat and other Scythic invaders in the fifth century, and the real kindred of their Afghan conquerors; a supposition which is strongly supported by language and family likeness, as well as by identity of manners and customs, and quick amalgamation.

For many years after this, the tenure of their conquest was a constant source of trouble to the Yúsufzai, owing to the persistent efforts made by the expelled Dalazak to recover their lost lands; until, finally, as the cause of tumult and disorder, they were deported *en masse* by the Emperor Jehangír, and distributed over different parts of Hindustan and Dakhan (Deccan). There are still some scattered families of this people in the Peshawar, Chach, and Paklí districts, and there is said to be a colony of about four hundred families of them settled in Dholpúr. In the time of their prosperity in Peshawar they were in two great factions named Gári and Gaúmat; but these are not now known, though the terms point to a division of the people as to creed-profession—of Zoroastrianism and Brahmanism.

The Yúsufzai accounts of this conquest are interspersed with many amusing incidents, and the record of some remarkable feats of bravery, together with descriptions of their arms and military engines, for, at that time, fire-arms were unknown to them. Amongst the list of their heroic exploits, it is related how one of their young warriors leapt his horse across the Gaúhar rivulet, at a point where it flowed mid-plain between steeply scarped banks, and, putting to flight hundreds of the infidel crew, slew their champion who stood to fight. And, it is added, when the victor cut off his adversary's head "as much beer flowed from the cursed pagan's throat as blood."

The ruse by which the Yúsufzai gained possession of Swat is graphically described by their historian and high priest, the Akhúnd Darweza Bábá, in his Tathkira or "Memoirs." He relates how the Yúsufzai sent their women and drummers with standards and tents to the foot of the easy Malakand pass to make demonstrations of forcing it, whilst their warriors entered the valley by the difficult and undefended one of Skakot. The Swatis, finding the enemy in the heart of their country, fled in all directions to the fastnesses of their mountains, and from those inaccessible retreats, for twelve years, maintained an obstinate guerilla warfare; till, finally, the calamity of a dreadful famine drove them to submission, after they had for a considerable time subsisted on the corpses of their own dead. With the subjection of this people the two great divisions of the Yúsufzai separated: Mandar holding the plain country, and Mali the mountains. The natives who remained, meanwhile, became converted to Islám, lost their identity of race, and were called Swátí. It was not so, however, with those of them who fled the country, for though they also subsequently became Musalmáns they retained their original tribal names, as will be presently mentioned.

Whilst the Yúsufzai were carrying on the war on the plain country before defined, their kinsmen and allies, the Mahmand, were prosecuting their conquest with equal success in the hill country between the Kabul and Swat rivers—in the true Gandhár. They crossed the former river at Dháka, and in the first instance established themselves in the Goshtá district. Here they were soon attacked by a people called Gandhárí (Gandharai in the singular) from the hills to the eastward. The contest thus begun proved fierce and prolonged, till at last the Mahmand, favoured by the operations of the Yúsufzai in the plains on the Peshawar side, forced their way into the heart of the country to Gandhár, its principal town. The name still exists as that of a considerable village or township, as well as of the district in which it stands, and the original inhabitants are still called Gandhárí in distinction to the Mahmand conquerors.

From this central seat of the natives the conquerors descended into the plain, in the angle between the junction of the Swat and Kabul rivers. Subsequently they crossed the latter river, and established themselves along the hill skirts up to the Bára river, in front of the Afrídí hills. In their victorious war with the natives the Mahmand appear to have acted with such fierce barbarity that the majority fled the country, and, crossing the Kunar river, found refuge and escape, among an apparently kindred people, in the fastnesses of Kama and Katár (Kafiristan), and in the valleys opening from them upon the Kabul river as far west as Tagáo.

For some considerable period these fugitive Gandhárí retained their original religion and customs, and were styled by the Muhammadans *Káfir* or "Infidel." Gradually, however, as Islám made its slow and steady progress among the neighbouring pagan peoples, they, or at least a large proportion of them who were in direct territorial contact with Musalmáns, accepted the Muhammadan creed, first passing through the intermediate stage of *Nímcha*, or "Half-and-Half," that is, half Kafir and half Musalmán; for owing to their position between and dealings with the Musalmáns on one side, and the Kafir on the other, they were Kafir to the Kafir, and Musalmán with the Musalmán; and this was owing to the jealousy of each for his own religion. As Islám secured its foothold, the Nimcha became strong enough to become the full Musalmán without the fear of vengeance from the Pagan. So long as they remained Nimcha or Kafir, they were simply known by those terms, but when they became Musalmán, they were distinguished by the original patronymics of the race. Thus, whilst the fugitive Gandhárí, who still remain pagans, are known only as Kafir, distinguished sometimes by the names of the localities they inhabit (such as, the Kafir Kamoji in Káma, Katárí or Katori in Katár or Kator), those who have become Musalmáns are distinguished by their original tribal names. Thus the converted Gandhárí are now divided into two great sections, named Sáfi and Gandhárí. Together they number about twelve thousand families, who are scattered about in small parties all over the country from Swat and Bájawar to Lughmán and Tagáo. In most places they occupy a dependant or servile position, and are counted faithful servants and good soldiers. Being recent converts, they are extremely bigoted and fanatical, and furnish many aspirants to the Muhammadan priesthood, in the ranks of which some of them have risen to the dignity of saints. The late celebrated Akhund of Swat—Saint and King combined—was a Gandhárai, though he was generally called a Sáfai, because the latter name is commonly used by strangers as that of the two divisions of the people, just as the name Yúsufzai is commonly used for Yúsuf or Mandar, and Mali—the two great divisions of the people. The now famous Mulla Mushki Alam—priest and saint of Ghazni—who has made himself so prominent a champion of the Faith against us in the Kabul campaign, is said to be an Akhundzada originally of the Sáfi tribe; though now he is reckoned a Ghilzai of the Andar section, owing to his family having been settled amongst them for three or four generations.

It is curious to note the character of the warfare by which these returned Gandhárí recovered possession of their fatherland from their unrecognized kindred, who, retaining still their ancient creed and customs, were to them merely cursed infidels, and fair prey to the sword of Islám.

No less interesting is it to compare the aspect and condition of the country at the time of this conquest, with its flourishing state at the time of the first Muhammadan invasion, and that of its present prosperity under British rule.

It is a remarkable circumstance in the history of the march of these two Afghan tribes that they were nowhere seriously opposed on the road, and even traversed the now historic Khybar Pass without coming into collision with its Afrídí possessors, who were yet infidels, as is proved clearly by a very important piece of evidence, which will be mentioned in its proper place. The Yúsufzais probably compounded for a passage with the descendants of the neighbours of their own ancestors, and for a while remained stationary on the waste lands skirting the Khybar hills. Here quarrels ensued with the possessors of the country in respect to the use of its pastures and water channels, and the Yúsufzais, discovering their strength, soon took the offensive and forced their opponents to give way. It would appear that though the bulk of the natives were infidels, the provincial and district rulers were Musalmáns, and it is probable that it was owing to the support and countenance of these officials, that their invading co-religionists were enabled to carry their aggressive proceedings to a successful issue.

Be this as it may, the Yúsufzais, in the course of twenty years' warfare, completely conquered the country which now bears their name. And they found the country eminently adapted to their mode of warfare, moving as they did with their families and flocks, and possessing themselves of the pasture lands and townships as they advanced bit by bit.

The country was no longer the civilized, well regulated, populous, and highly prosperous kingdom that it was in the glorious era of the Budhist rule. The numerous ruins of its for mercities and ecclesiastical towns, its monasteries and topes, which cover the country by the score, are the mute and desolate witnesses of its former prosperity and populousness, of the industry of its people, and their civilized and peaceable mode of life. The excavations which have been made during recent years in the ruins of "Takht da Bahai"—the Pushtú for "Takhti Vihár" of the Persian, or in our language the "Monastery ridge"—have revealed much that is of historical and archæological interest, especially in the skill of the architect, and the delicacy and art of the sculptor, and the mode of domestic life of the inhabitants of the country in the years of its prosperity—from the second century before our era to the tenth or eleventh after it. Whilst the excavations in the ruins of Sáwaldher, Shahri Bahlol, and Jamálgarhí have increased our knowledge, and confirmed the opinion that the Indian sculptors were originally instructed by Greek masters, not a tithe, however, of the ruins of the country have been as yet touched. Swat, Bájáwar, and Buner, beyond the border, teem with these silent relics of the past, and the ruins of Nawágrám, Kharki, Paja, and many others, all within our border, wait to tell their tale so soon as any one will examine them.

It is the number of these monuments of past ages which

serve to guide us in our estimate of the former prosperity and fulness of life of the country in which they are found. That prosperity has passed away with the advent of Islám—with its blighting and destructive influences, its bigoted and intolerant law, and its stagnant or retrograde rule.

During the closing years of the tenth and early years of the succeeding century of our era, Mahmúd, the first Sultan and Musalmán of the Turk dynasty of kings who ruled at Ghazni, made a succession of inroads, twelve or fourteen in number, into Gandhár—the present Peshawar valley—in the course of his proselytizing invasions of Hindustan. He was a fierce bigot and arch destroyer. Fire and sword, havoc and destruction, marked his course everywhere. Gandhár, which was styled the "Garden of the North," was left at his death a weird and desolate waste. Its rich fields and fruitful gardens, together with the canal which watered them (the course of which is still partially traceable in the western part of the plain), had all disappeared. Its numerous stone-built cities, monasteries, and topes, with their valuable and revered monuments and sculptures, were sacked, fired, razed to the ground, and utterly destroyed as habitations.

Left in this state of devastation and depopulation, the country soon grew into a wilderness, the haunt of wild beasts, and the refuge of robbers. The fugitive inhabitants, returning in small numbers to their destroyed homes, gradually re-peopled the country and reclaimed bits of the waste. But their numbers were greatly reduced, and the impression they made upon the desolation worked by their Muhammadan enemies was hardly perceptible, owing to the distances at which their restored villages were scattered. The country was overgrown with jungle, and overrun with wild beasts. The wolf, leopard, and tiger hunted the herds of antelope which had made their home in the wilderness, and the rhinoceros wallowed in the marshes that covered the hill skirt to the north and terminated in a small lake not far from the Indus at Topi.

Such was the state of the country when the Yúsufzais during the rule at Kabul of Mirza Ulugh Beg—about the middle of the fifteenth century—entered upon its conquest. They seem to have reclaimed much of the waste, and, abandoning their nomadic life, to have quickly settled down in village communities as agriculturalists. The change in their mode of life and the cessation of wars had the natural effect of greatly increasing their numbers, and multiplying their wealth in cattle and flocks. So much so that, in the middle of the sixteenth century, when the Emperor Babur passed through their country on his way to Delhi, they were considered an important and powerful people. Babur considered their chief of sufficient rank to enter into alliance with him, to marry his daughter, and to take a contingent of twelve thousand of his tribesmen as an addition to his army. The Emperor in his quaint and valuable memoirs records some interesting incidents of his progress through the Peshawar valley, and among them mentions having hunted the rhinoceros at the mouth of the Khybar and in the Razar marsh before alluded to, and also the tiger at what is now the Attock ferry across the Indus. Both the tiger and the rhinoceros have long since disappeared from this country. But it would appear that the latter was in former centuries a very common animal in the Razar marshes, for an adjacent pass and valley bear the name of Ambela (the scene of the campaign of that name in 1863-64 against the Wahábi fanatics), which is the antique Persian word for rhinoceros.

Jumping to conclusions from mere names, however, is not a safe course, but in this instance the corroborating circumstances favour the notion that the localities derived their names from the animals which are known to have haunted them. As an instance of the danger of drawing conclusions from mere names, it may be here stated that the Yúsufzais reckon themselves true Afghans and call themselves Bani Isráíl. Their name means "descendants of Joseph," and their country abounds with Israelitish names such as are found in the Scriptures. In fact, by the hasty enquirer, their claims would be at once admitted, and their country be considered a second Palestine; for in support of the belief there is the hill Peor (Pehor), the mount Moriah (Morah), the peaks of Ilam and Dumah, the valley of Sodom (Sudhum), the stream of the Gadarenes (Gadhar), the plain of Galilee (Jalala), &c., for places; whilst for tribes there are the Amazites (Amazai), the Moabites (Muhibwál), the Hittites (Hotiwál), &c.

After this it appears the Yúsufzais increased considerably in population, and brought wide tracts of the wilderness under cultivation, but still not to such an extent as to effect any marked change in the general desolate aspect of the country. This was partly owing to their village feuds and fights for the fair division of the pasture lands, and partly to their wars with another people, who, like themselves, had recently emigrated from their native country further west, and settled in the territory adjoining that of the Yúsufzais, but on the south side of the Kabul river. The name of this tribe was Khattak, and though they were Pukhtána, or Pathán, they were not Afghan. They will be treated of separately later on. Here it may be stated that in their contests with the Yúsufzai they were by no means unsuccessful, for they managed to possess themselves of two most important strategic positions in the Yúsufzai country, which they hold to the present day. In order to put a stop to the cattle-lifting forays of the Yúsufzais, from which it appears they suffered great loss, they crossed the Kabul river, and possessed themselves of the belt of land on its north bank from the point of junction of the Swat with the Kabul river to that of the latter with the Indus at Attock. But this position did not protect them from the constant forays of the Yúsufzais, especially of their raiding parties from Swat and Buner. The Khattaks were consequently forced to adopt measures to protect themselves from this source of annoyance and danger. They pushed a military colony straight across the plain, and taking up a position which commanded the approach to Swat on one side, and to Buner on the other, there firmly established themselves. This spot is now called Jamálgarhi, and lies at the base of the Pajah hill. It is still in the possession of the descendants of the original colonists.

We need not here follow the history of the Yúsufzais during the reigns of the successive Mughal Emperors, nor need we waste time in the relation of their home feuds and wars, nor of their stubborn opposition to the conquering Sikhs. It will be enough for our purpose to close this account of them by a brief notice of their present condition. The arid wastes and the turbulent people we took over from the Sikhs on the conquest of the Panjab in 1849, are now, after a brief thirty years of British rule, no longer the same, either in the aspect of the country or in the condition of the people. The wide plain which was formerly traversed by uncertain tracks is now crossed in all directions by good roads. The cattle-guards, armed to the teeth with an odd variety of weapons, who used formerly to take post on the numerous mounds of the ancient Budhist topes and tumuli, and from their tops scan the wide expanse on all sides against the raider and robber, are now no longer known, and their place is taken by boys whose only weapon is a club or an ox-goad. The plain which was formerly mostly wilderness and uninhabited, is now dotted over with prosperous village communities, and cultivation has spread to such an extent that the cattle are hard put to for pasture in some localities. Lastly, the fanatic and turbulent Yúsufzai of thirty years ago, though still fanatical, is a very altered man from his unreclaimed and independent brother in the hill parts of the country. He is now by no means the restless and troublesome fellow he was in his poverty and ignorance of only twelve or fifteen years ago. He is now grown wealthy, luxurious, and as loyal to the British Government, under whose beneficent rule he has acquired these personal advantages and blessings, as any other people in India.

CHAPTER VIII.

THE AFRIDI.

The Afrídí (or Afridai in the singular) are without doubt the present representatives of the Aparytæ of Herodotus. Both the names and the positions are identically the same. The extent of the ancient country and the character of its people appear to have undergone a considerable change, but still not so great as to mar identity. The original limits of the Afrídí (or Afreedee, as the name is often spelt) country, probably, comprised the whole of the Sufed Koh range and the country at the base of it on the north and south sides—to the Kabul and Kurram rivers respectively—whilst its extent from east to west was from the Pewár ridge, or the head waters of the Kurram further west, to the Indus, between the points of junction with it of the Kabul and Kurram rivers, in the former direction.

With the Afrídí of the present day are now reckoned as kindred tribes the Orakzai and Bangash, of whose origin very little is known, though they are, perhaps, of Scythic descent, and came into their present positions with the Scythic irruption before alluded to. By the Afghans they are classed as Turklánrí, which is a division of the Ghurghusht tribe of Afghans. The Ghurghusht tribe is held to be composed of the descendants of the third son of Kais—the great ancestral progenitor of the Pukhto-speaking peoples—and will be again referred to hereafter.

The Turklánrí people, according to the Afghan writers, include the Afrídí, Orakzai, Bangash, Tori, Wazírí, &c., &c.,

who are mostly settled in the northern half of the Sulemán range. The word itself means "the Turk brotherhood" or "kinsfolk," just as *Khorlánrí* means "sisterhood," or the affinity between sisters or maidens associated together; but there seems to be some confusion in the tribes so put together, as the list includes also the Khattak and several petty Indian tribes on the north of the Kabul river, as well as the Jájí and others to the south of it, and to the west of the Khybar.

The Turklánrí are also known by the names of Kararai or Karalánrí (the *n* is nasal); and the story connected with their origin is to the effect that, two brothers of the Khattak tribe were on the march together when they came upon the camping ground of an army which had recently left it. The one brother who was childless, found an iron cooking-pot, called *karrhai* in Pukhtú, and the other, who was over blessed with children, found an infant boy amongst the refuse of the camp. The brothers exchanged their windfalls, and the boy was called in connection with the above circumstances Kararai, which afterwards, as the tribes sprung from him increased in numbers and power, was changed to Karalánrí. The drift of the legend indicates the invasion of foreigners, and their settlement in the country, but the absence of dates and particulars leaves their identification altogether uncertain, especially as no locality is indicated. From the mention of the Khattak people, however, it would seem that the Turklánrí were composed of various sects of different Turk tribes who successively came into these parts with the invasions of Sabaktakin in the tenth, and of Tymur in the sixteenth centuries of our era. They very probably maintained their national identity till the collapse of the Chaghatai or Tymur dynasty, after which they lost power and became absorbed into the general nationality of the country. It seems certain, also, that some Turk tribes came down and settled on the Sulemán range at a much earlier period than the time of Sabaktakin, for the early Arab historians mention the fact of their armies being opposed by a Turk people in the country now held by the Kákar. This was in the first century of the Muhammadan, and eighth of our own era, and the facts alluded to may probably be relegated to the Scythic invasion already mentioned. The subject is one well deserving careful investigation.

Whatever the origin of the Orakzai and Bangash, they appear to have shifted from their first positions in this country, for the Bangash are stated to have been originally settled in Zurmal or Zurmat, next to the Katti of Kattawáz. Here they were constantly at feud with their neighbours, the Farmuli, as well as amongst themselves, the two great national factions of Sámal and Gára being always at war. They were ousted from Zurmat, say the Afghan accounts, about five hundred years ago, by the Ghilji, and driven into Kurram, and, finally, after a prolonged contest there with the Tori, they were forced into their present position in Miránzai and Kohát. Many of these tribes, however, emigrated to Hindustan, where the Orakzai established a colony at Bhopál, and the Bangash another at Farukhábád in the North-West Provinces. The family of the present Nawab of Farukhábád belongs to this tribe, as does that of the Begam of Bhopál to the Orakzai.

The Afrídí country, it would thus appear, was at an early period encroached upon by a variety of petty Turk tribes, and the natives, unable to withstand them, retired to the interior of their mountains, to Tírah and Mydán, and to the fastnesses of the Khybar hills, in short, to the hilly country which extends from the main range of Sufed Koh to the Indus. The tract lying to the south of this, from Mydan in the west to the Indus at Karabagh in the east, was held mainly by Orakzai, whilst the Miranzai and Kurram valleys were held by the Bangash. A division of the ancient Afrídí country, after something of this sort, held good, it appears, till about six or seven hundred years ago, when the original inhabitants were ousted by encroaching tribes entirely foreign to the country, and of distinct race. Thus the traditions of the Torís of the Kurram valley trace their arrival in the present seat of their people from northern Sind, where they formed a powerful section of the Toghiani Turks. And the date of their conquest they carry back to some six hundred years ago. It was about this time also that the ancient neighbours of the Aparytæ, being driven from their native seats, forced themselves into the Aparytæ territories, and, under the name of Khattak, established themselves in all the country from the lower Kabul river on the north to the Kurram on the south.

It would thus appear that the Afrídí of to-day holds but a small portion of the territory assigned above as the possession of his ancient progenitors, the Aparytæ mentioned by Herodotus. The northern base of Sufed Koh is now in the possession of several different tribes of whom the Ghiljí, the Khogiani, and the Shinwarí are the principal. The latter people whose proper name is Shirwáni are the latest new arrivals in these parts, and are said to have come from the Persian Shirwán in the time of Nadír Shah. They have mostly lost their own language, and have adopted that and the manners and customs of the Patháns. They occupy the western end of the Khybar Pass and the adjoining valleys on the northern base of Sufed Koh. They are a fine race of people of different physique to their neighbours, and are the great carriers of this part of the country between Kabul and Peshawar. Their mules and donkeys are of superior breed and much in demand both at Kabul and Peshawar. The Shinwari is considered a good soldier and a clever robber.

The southern base of the Sufed Koh is now in the possession of the Toris, before mentioned, and the Khostwáls, who appear to be an allied tribe; whilst the whole of the Indus *riverain*, between the Kabul and Kurram rivers, as far westwards as Kohat and Bahadur Khel, is held by the Khattaks.

All that now remains to the Afrídí and his ancient joint partners in the territory assigned to the Aparytæ is the heart of the country—the Kohat Pass and valley, the Khybar Pass and hills, the Miranzai valley, and the uplands at the eastern end of the Sufed Koh range. In the south-west corner of this central tract is located a small and obscure tribe, the Zymukht, supposed to be Afghans, and celebrated mostly as expert and desperate robbers.

The Afrídí, Orakzai, Bangash, Khattak, Tori, Zymukht, Khostwál, Jáji or Zázi, Mangal, &c., tribes are all classed together under two political factions known by the name of Sámal and Gár or Gára, respectively. The factions are of no political importance nowadays, though of great interest as a guide to the former affinities and relations of their respective members. The people themselves have not the smallest idea of the origin of the opposite factions under which, as a matter of hereditary duty, they are enrolled; yet they are very tenacious of the distinction, and never change from one to the other. The factions, evidently, came into existence on the conversion of the people *en bloc* to Islám, when all became a common brotherhood in the faith, and called themselves Musulmáns, though yet they maintained a distinction expressive of their original religious separation—a sign that their conversion was effected by force, and was more nominal than real at first. And thus the peoples of the two rival religions at that time flourishing side by side in this region—namely the Budhist and the Magian—ranged themselves naturally under the respective standards or factions of their original religions; the Budhist Sáman or Sráman giving the name to the one, and the Magian Gabr, Gaur or Gár to the other.

Looking at the Afrídí as we find him to-day, it is difficult to imagine him the descendant of the mild, industrious, peace-loving, and contemplative Budhist, abhorrent of the shedding of blood or the destruction of life of even the minutest or meanest of God's creatures; or even to imagine him descended from fire-worshipping ancestors, whose tender care for life was almost equal to that of the Budhist, and whose sincere and punctilious devotion to the observance of the minute ceremonies and ordinances of their religion was surpassed by none. The Afrídí of to-day, though professedly a Muhammadan, has really no religion at all. He is, to a great extent, ignorant of the tenets and doctrines of the creed he professes, and even if he knew them, would in no way be restrained by them in pursuit of his purpose.

Whatever he may have been as a Budhist, or as a Fire-worshipper, he has now sunk to the lowest grade of civilization, and borders upon the savage. Entirely illiterate, under no acknowledged control, each man his own king, the nation has dwindled down to a small community of less than three hundred thousand souls, mostly robbers and cut-throats, without principles of conduct of any kind, and with nothing but the incentive of the moment as the prompter to immediate action. Even among his own nationality (the Patháu) he is accounted the faithless of the faithless, and is held on all sides to be the most fierce and stealthy of all enemies. As we know him, merely in the character of an independent neighbour, he is a wily, mistrusting, wolfish, and wilful savage, with no other object in life but the pursuit of robbery and murder, and the feuds they give rise to.

His ignorance and barbarism are a bye-word among neighbour tribes, and many amusing stories are told against them. One to the effect that, although professedly Musalmáns, they showed no reverence for the Mulla, or Muhammadan priest, and plundered and despitefully used the too confiding members of the profession who ventured among them so impartially, that their country was soon shunned by the whole clergy class as a dangerous place. Thus neglected in religious training they became a laughing-stock to their better instructed co-religionists in the plain country, and through shame they were driven to entice a zealous "Mulla" of the Peshawar city to their mountain home. The priest installed in his new place, as in duty bound to do, urged upon his untutored flock the great advantages to be derived from the pilgrimage to the sacred shrines of saints and martyrs for the Faith, and enlarged upon the untold benefits that followed upon the offerings there made in the name of the Saint. This was enough for the Afrídí mind. He was to gain advantages by making visits to sacred shrines and depositing offerings in the name of the saints to whom they were dedicated to propitiate their favour and protection, and he determined to make pilgrimages and offerings. But there was not such a thing as a "Ziyárat" in the whole country, and to go to the sacred shrines in the territories of their neighbours was not to be thought of, for the Afrídí's hand was against everybody, and everybody's hand was against the Afrídí. In this dilemma, what easier than to have a "Ziyárat" in their own country, and who more suitable as a martyr for the faith than their venerable priest. So the "Mulla" was sacrified, and a "Ziyárat" raised over his remains, and Tiráh had its first sacred shrine. Perhaps it is the only one, for the Afrídí is no ways noted for any devotion to this form of piety.

The Afghan account of the Afrídí genealogy indicates his long ancestry, for they derive him from nobody, and to account for his name have concocted a feeble story, which, however, is highly characteristic of the pride of race of the whole tribe. The story goes—that in ancient times some Governor of the province of Peshawar summoned some members of the tribe to his "Darbar," or Court of Audience. One of them, with native self-possession and independence, took his seat at the entrance to the darbar, and as the Governor approached to enter his Court, made no move to rise. The Governor stopped, and asked him who he was. *Dzah tsok yam?*—"Who am I?"—he replied with stolid indifference, *Dzah hum Afridai yam*—

"I also am a creature of God!" In the Persian *Afrida* means "a created being." From this circumstance the tribe received the name of Afrídí.

As our immediate independent neighbours during thirty years of British rule on the Trans-Indus frontier, the Afrídís, or Khybaris, as they are often called from their holding (until only the other day) possession of that famous pass, have given us great and almost continuous trouble. Their bold robberies in the very centre of our Peshawar cantonments, with its garrison of eight thousand men, have passed into the stock history of the place. Their highway robberies and murders, and their village raids and cattle-lifting forays brought them into constant collision with our frontier officers. The result of thirty years' contact with them has in no way attached the people to us, nor has the example of British rule made any visible change in their condition, except perhaps in enabling them, through our own neglect to protect ourselves manfully, to become the best armed of any of our frontier tribes. We shall have some day to conquer this people and annex the country, and we shall then find what a born race of marksmen can do with our own Enfields and Sniders and Martini Henri's in their hands—partly acquired by a weakness the Afrídí has for enlisting into our Native Army and then deserting, and, quite naturally, taking his arms with him; but mostly by clever theft in the barracks of every newly-arrived regiment, European or Native.

CHAPTER IX.

THE KHATTAK.

THE Sattagydæ of Herodotus are identified in the Saitak, Sattak, Shattak, and Khattak of modern native writers. The two last forms are merely the western and eastern modes, respectively, of Pushtú pronunciation. Their original seat was on the Sulemán range and its great western off shoot, called Koh Sauwál, and the plain country down to the Indus as far south as the present Dehra Ismail Khan. On the Sulemán range their limit to the south ended at Barmal, and marched with the Kákar frontier. At a very early period the Khattaks were, it appears, driven out of the plain country on the Indus by the Waziri tribe, who, after a long lapse of time, being themselves pressed in rear by other tribes from Sind, were forced forward, and pushing themselves into the hill country of the Khattaks, dispossessed that ancient people of their original home. This is said to have occurred about six hundred years ago. At some considerable period prior to this, however, it appears that the Khattaks were invaded from the west by a Persian people now commonly known by the name of Chakmani or Chamkani. This people did not conquer or dispossess the Khattaks, but settled in the country amongst them, mostly in and about their principal towns of Mukím and Kánígoram. Though all this country is now in the hands of the Waziris, there are still three or four hundred houses of the Chamkani dwelling in these two towns as subjects of the Waziri.

The Chamkani, it appears, were a heretical sect of Persian Islamites, and fled their own country on account of the persecutions of the Government. They are said to have belonged (for they are now orthodox Musalmáns) to the sect of Shíá Muhammadans called Ali Ilahi on account of their belief in the divinity of Ali, the son-in-law of Muhammad. Curious stories are told of their peculiar religious ceremonies and immoral proceedings connected with them. A burning light, it appears, was an essential element in their religious performances, in which both sexes joined indiscriminately, and at a particular stage of the ceremonies and recitations it was extinguished by the officiating priest. On this signal the congregation fell to the orgies and immoralities of which they are accused. On account of this strange custom they were called by the Persians *chirágh-kush* and by the Patháns *or-mur*, which mean respectively "lamp-extinguisher" and "fire-extinguisher." Their great ancestor or leader in these parts was one Amr Lobán, but nothing more is recorded of him than his name. According to Afghan accounts this people were dispersed about five hundred years ago in consequence of a famine which raged in their country for three or four years. Some of them moved into the Logar valley, south of Kabul, where they settled at Barkibarak; others emigrated to the Peshawar valley, where the village of Chamkani marks their settlement; others again went on into Hindustan, and there became lost in the general population of the country. A considerable number, however, held to their homes in Kánígoram and Mukím; and others to their settlements on the north border of the country, where they had as neighbours the petty tribes of Mangal and Khitáí and Zázaí—evidently immigrant tribes from Mangalái and Khitái (our Cathay) in North-Western China. The total number of the Chamkani is reckoned at about five thousand families. They are considered a quiet, inoffensive, and industrious people, and distinguished as the only tribe in these parts not given to feudal fights and highway robbery.

On being turned out of their own country by the Waziri,

the Khattaks, together with some of their neighbours of the Haní and Mangal tribes, are said to have retreated to the Banú territory, and settled at Doyál, which was called also Sadráwan. Here they quarrelled with their stranger comrades and expelled them from their midst. After this the Khattaks were attacked by the Baloch, and forced to go north-east to the Koh Khingán. From this they gradually spread by Karbogha, Terí, Chautra, Lácha, &c., to the Indus. Whilst the Khattaks were thus working their way eastward, the Bangash were being driven out of Kurram by the Tori, who, it seems, were advancing from the south-east diagonally across the route by which the Khattaks had come. The Bangash, on their part, being ousted from their possessions in Kurram, fell back upon their allied tribe, the Orakzai, and contested the land with them. Whilst they were thus engaged in hostilities, the Khattak took the opportunity to extend their lands to Tora Chapra and Patiala at the expense of the Orakzai, and thus became neighbours of the Bangash, a hill ridge between Lácha and Gadákhel being the separating boundary, which it is to this day. Gradually as the Khattaks increased in strength, they extended northward, and pressing aside the Orakzai and Afrídí to the higher hills, took possession of all the Indus riverain up to the Kabul river, and even advanced across it, as before mentioned, into the Yúsufzai country. In their advance they absorbed several small communities of foreign settlers, such as the Mughalki and Síní (Mughal or Mongol, and Chinese), whom they include in their Búlác division, and the Jalozai, Dangarzai, and Oriyákhel, whom they include in their Terí division.

The Khattak, with whom are included the Banúchí, are physically a fine race, and differ from all other Patháns in features, general appearance, and many of their customs. They are also distinguished from the other eastern Patháns, as being the only tribe amongst them who speak the soft or western dialect of Pushtú. The Afghan account of the origin of their name, whilst illustrative of the manners of the people in the olden times, shows the simplicity of mind of their descendants, and their entire reliance for information upon their priests; for having themselves lost all trace of their ancestry they are fain to believe whatever their spiritual masters choose to tell them.

The story goes that one day four brothers (it does not say of what tribe) went out for a stroll or to hunt on the plain (locality not specified), and as they went on they saw, as they knew by their dress, four young damsels coming their way. As they approached, the eldest brother said—"What better sport than this; let each of us take one of these damsels to wife!" His proposal was applauded, and they agreed to cast lots for them. The eldest brother, however, claimed his right of seniority to take his choice without casting lots, and this was conceded to him. By this time the approaching parties met, and the eldest brother stopping the damsels, selected the most gaily dressed as his choice. The others were apportioned by lot. When all were distributed, each brother unveiled his damsel, and it was discovered that the one in the finest and gaudiest clothes was a shrivelled-up ugly old maid, whilst the others in more simple and sober attire were comely young virgins. The more fortunate younger brothers laughing twitted the other on his bad taste in selecting such a bride, and repeating a phrase commonly used on occasions of like misadventure, said—"*Pa khatta lárye,*" that is, "You've gone into the mud," or, as we should say, "You've put your foot in it." From this incident, says the Afghan genealogist, is derived the name of Khattak; and then he goes on to add, that from each of the four damsels sprung a numerous progeny, who increased and multiplied and gave their names to all the sections and sub-divisions of the tribe. Under British rule the Khattak has proved a generally well-conducted and loyal subject. The salt mines of Kalabagh are in their hands, and many of them are employed as travelling merchants and salt carriers to the mountainous region between the Peshawar valley and Badakhshan. The chief of the Khattaks, Khwaja Muhammad Khan, was made a Knight of the Order of the Star of India a few years ago in recognition of his loyalty and services to Government.

The WAZIRI who displaced the Khattak, or Shattak, as it is pronounced in the western dialect of Pushtú, from his ancient seat on the Sulemán range, from the Sattagydia of Herodotus, for he is the only one of the ancient authors who has mentioned this people, appear to be identical with the Wairsí or Vairsí of the early Muhammadan historians. The Wairsí were a division of the Sodha tribe, which itself was a branch of the Pramára Rájpút. The Waziri appear to have made their first assaults against the Khattak about five or six hundred years ago at a time when the country was sorely afflicted with famine; and the route they took was across the Sham plain into the adjoining valley and district of Barmal. Here they settled and remained for some time before making a further forward move. In Barmal is the favourite shrine of an ancestral and saintly chief of the tribe, and here also are the lands of one of the tribal sub-divisions named Sodhaki. From their settlement in Barmal, the Waziri advanced by degrees, and in a long course of years, driving the Khattak before them, and subjugating the Chamkani, took the whole of the ancient Khattak country from the Sham plain on the south, to the Kohat valley in the north.

They are a powerful and entirely independent tribe, and mostly pastoral and nomade in their habits of life. In personal appearance they are very different from other Pathán tribes, and retain many customs peculiar to themselves. On the western borders of their territory they share the pasture lands with the Sulemán-Khel, Kharoti, and other sections of the great Ghilzai tribe.

CHAPTER X.

THE DADICÆ.

THE DADICÆ are the last of the four Indian nations mentioned by Herodotus as forming a single Satrapy on the extreme eastern frontier of the Empire of Darius. There has been some difference of opinion as to the identification of this people. By one party they are supposed to be represented by the modern Tájik, but this does not seem a natural philological transition; and besides the term Tájik only came into common use after the Arab conquest of Persia, as will be explained further on when we come to consider the Tájik people. Others, again, have considered them to be represented by the hill people located north of the Gandarians, and formerly called Darada, a name which is still known to, but not in common use amongst, that people, though it is still the patronymic of the natives of Chilas, on the other side of the Indus, who style themselves Dárd. The transition from Darada to Dadicæ is not a natural one either, and it is much more probable that the Dadicæ, who were evidently neighbours of the Sattagydæ, are truly represented by the existing Dádí, a small tribe now incorporated with the Kákar, and still clinging to their ancient seat. The Dadicæ or Dádí, it would appear, originally possessed all the country now occupied by the different clans composing the Kákar tribe, but were gradually ousted, decimated, and finally absorbed by them. When these changes took place it is difficult to say, but the subject will be better understood if we leave the Dádí, and turn to the consideration of the Kákar, the present possessors of the country.

The Kákar of Afghanistan are a people of Scythic origin, and of kindred race with the Gakkar or Ghakkar, who are settled in Chach and Rawal Pindi on the other side of the Indus, and other parts of India. According to the Afghan accounts, Kákar was the grandson of Ghurghusht or Ghirghisht, by his second son, Dání. And this Ghirghisht was the youngest of the three sons of Kais or Kish, the great ancestral progenitor of the Afghan nationality of modern times. It has already been shown how the name of the first son, Saraban, was merely the adoption of the race title of the people whom the Afgan genealogists classified together as one set of the descendants of Kais, and the fact of their Rájpút origin might have been then made clearer by tracing up to more recent times, the names of the successive generations of ancestors, except that it would needlessly complicate the subject by a multiplicity of strange names. At the risk of this, however, it may be here mentioned that the above-named Saraban, according to the Afghan genealogies, had two sons named Sharjyún and Khrishyún. These are evidently transformations of the common Rájpút proper names—Surjan and Krishan; and they have been still more altered by transformation into Muhammadan names—Sharjyún being changed into Sharfuddín and Krishyún into Khyruddín. Similar traces of Indian affinity are to be found in almost all the Afghan genealogical tables. And it is only what we might expect when we remember the tradition that the five Pándú brother kings, about the time of the Mahabhárat, or great war which was decided on the field of Kuru Kshetr, near Thanesar north of Delhi, emigrated to the Panjab and Afghanistan as far as Ghazni and Kandahar, and there established independent kingdoms which lasted for several centuries. The third son of Kais, Ghirghisht or Ghurghusht, appears to have derived his name from the national origin of the clans classed together as his descendants by Afghan genealogists, in the same way as they have done with the name of the eldest son, Saraban. For

Ghirghisht, it appears, is only an altered form of Cirghiz or Ghirghiz—"wanderer on the steppe"—and indicates the country whence the people originally came, namely northern Turkistan. For Cirghiz or Kirghiz merely means a wanderer or nomade in the language of that country, and corresponds with the more familiar term Scythian. Though the Kákar now holds the greater portion of the ancient Dadicæ country by a number of clans confederated under his own name, they are not all of the same origin as himself. For the other sons of Dání (after whom, in the early Muhammadan period, the northern part of the present Kákar country was named Dánistan, as the southern was named Kákarán or Kákaristán), namely Dádí, Nághar, and Paní, are expressly distinguished in Afghan histories, as differing, in many of their manners and customs, as well as in dialect, from the true Kákar. Thus the Nághar are expressly designated as Rájpúts, and by the Afghans are commonly called Baroh. They are described as closely allied in origin and domestic customs, as well as in political relations, with the Paní; and they both have most of their clans settled in Shekhawáti and Hydarábád, the lesser parts only residing in Kákar territory. As to the Dádí, their history is lost in the obscurity to which they have sunk, and nothing more seems to be known about them now than that they have become absorbed into the Kákar tribe, and attached themselves to an immigrant colony from Khojand, with whom they are generally known as Khojandí or Khundí.

Besides the clans confederated with them in their own country, the Kákar claim kinship with the Gadún of Mahabán and Chach, on both sides the Indus north of Attock. These people on their part call themselves Kákar, and in Chach one of their settlements is called Ghurghusht. They also claim kinship with the Tymaní Cháráymác, who are settled in the Síah-band range of the Ghor mountains, to the south-east of Herat. This people, on their part, consider themselves a branch of the Kákar, and hold themselves separate from the rest of the Cháráymác further north, from whom they differ in manners and customs, as well as dialect and religion—these being Sunní and those Shía. The Tymani are in two divisions, one of which is called Capchác, who are Aymác or "nomade," and the other Darzi, who are settled, and are usually called Afghan.

The Kákar country on the Indus frontier is about a hundred miles square, and extends from the Waziri border on the north to the Baloch border on the south. The country is traversed from north to south by a mountain range, on the east and west slopes of which are many pleasant and fertile valleys. In the Kanjoghí valley, which runs about thirty miles south-west from the Kand peak, is settled the Sanya clan, and in Borí, an extensive valley running to the south-east, are the Sanjara and Sambhira clans—names evidently of Indian origin. The Kákar, in fact, is a collection of several different peoples, who, though now all speaking Pushtú and calling themselves Kákar Puthán, nevertheless maintain their own peculiar customs, manners, and dialects.

The bulk of the Kákar Proper are employed in the asafœtida trade between Herat and India; but most of the other clans lead a pastoral life, moving from place to place with their cattle and flocks, and living in small societies of three or four families, who pitch their black hair tents, or *Kizhdi*, in little clusters together. The lesser number are settled in villages and cultivate the soil in the main valleys, as Borí, Zhób, Kanjoghí, &c., &c. The Zhob range separates the Kákar from the Waziri. Their neighbours on the north-west are the Ghiljí, on the west the Achakzí, and on the south-west the Tarín—both Durrani tribes. On the south are the Baloch, the hereditary foe of the Kákar. The Shayúna Dágh, a mountain plateau, in the north-west of the country, is a celebrated pasture ground of the Kákar; and to the west of the Toba mountain they have a number of narrow little valleys whose several streams combine to form the Lohra river which waters the Peshín valley. In spring and summer the whole of this part of the country is said to be a delightful residence, the climate salubrious, and the air perfumed with the odours of the flowers which cover the surface as with a variegated carpet. The country is good, it is the people only who are bad, for they are ignorant, brutal, and savage in their manners, and robbers by intuition, as indeed are all the independent Pathán tribes.

We have thus shown that the Pathán comprises not only the modern representatives of the four ancient Pactiyan nations mentioned by Herodotus— to whom, alone indeed, the title properly belongs—but also a variety of other races, some kindred and some foreign, who have been thrown together within the area of their original country, the ancient Pactiya, by successive waves of conquest, and dynastic revolutions. All these different races, such as the Kákar, Waziri, Tori, &c., have evidently had a long struggle before they finally established themselves amongst the Pathán nations; and it would seem that it was only by blending with them, and, to some extent, adopting their manners and customs, that they were afterwards enabled not only to hold their own, but to enlarge their borders and maintain their distinct identity at the expense of the ancient inhabitants. The only other people of Afghanistan, besides those dwelling in the Pathán country proper, who call themselves Pathán, are the Afghan and the Ghilji. Apparently, simply because they, to a great extent, the latter especially, live within the limits of the Pathán country, and to some extent have adopted their language and social code of laws; and because it has pleased their genealogists to class them all together as a single nation descended from a common ancestral progenitor.

Until the recent changes, political and military—changes which are still in course of development on the Trans-Indus frontier of India—the Pathán tribes, who hold the mountain ranges of Sufed Koh and Sulemán Koh, have for the most part maintained their independence for many centuries; an independence, not of a united nation, but an independence of individual tribes. The Pathán tribes on the plains and low lands, between the mountains and the river, such as the Yúsufzai, the Khattak, Bangash, Banúchi, the Mahmand of the Peshawar valley, &c., have been British subjects ever since the conquest of the Panjab. Some of the hill tribes, such as those of the Kurram, Daur, and Síbí valleys, have been at different times, within the above period, subjugated by the Kabul Government. But all the powerful hill tribes, such as the Yúsufzai and Mahmand of the hills, the Wazírí, the Kákar, and several lesser tribes, are entirely independent, as are some clans of the hill Ghilzai.

From the foregoing account it would appear that the original Pactiyan, Pukhtún, or Pathán nations, though severally maintaining their identity to the present day, have become individually much mixed up with various tribes of foreigners brought into their midst by successive waves of conquest and revolution during many centuries. And this is just what we might expect, considering the situation of their country at the point of junction of the three great empires of the Persian, the Turk, and the Indian. How long it took for these different races to amalgamate into a nation speaking the same language, professing the same religion, and owning the same code of laws, it is difficult to say. But there is no doubt that the change once initiated was rapidly carried to completion; it would appear that in the accomplishment of this end, the influence of religion played an important part, and that the Budhist, Brahman, and Gabr, all simultaneously succumbed to the majesty of Islám. This religion was first systematically enforced upon the peoples of this country by the first Turk sovereign of that faith in these parts, the celebrated Mahmúd of Ghazni, about the beginning of the eleventh century. But however successful his means of fire and sword may have been at first, it appears that their effects were not very lasting nor complete. In short, the conversion of the people under such compulsion was only nominal, and they rapidly relapsed to their former creeds during the reigns of Mahúmd's successors, until in the time of Shahábuddín Ghori, the twelfth century, there occurred a revival of the Muhammadan religion all over India. About this time the whole Púkhtún country was overrun by Arab priests who assumed the title of Sayyid ("Lord"), and by native Indian converts, who were called Shekh ("Elder"). These enthusiastic propagandists seem to have set about the task of proselytizing the people with remarkable energy and boldness, though with no great self-denial or personal restraint. They everywhere made themselves very comfortable at free quarters amongst their ignorant flocks, freely took their daughters to wife, rigidly exacted the tithes and other offerings ordained by the law to their sacred callings, and punctiliously enforced the reverence and homage due to them as the expounders of the word of God and the guides to the delights of Paradise.

The priests of the Sunni or "orthodox" sect had not the field entirely to themselves, for they had already been preceded by those of the Persian Schismatics of the Shíá sect, as well as by the Persian heretics of the Ali Ilahi sect, who believed in the divinity of Ali. With the decline, however, of Persian influence in this quarter, they soon acquired the ascendancy, and the Shíá and the Ali Ilahi, or Chamkani, as he was called (the Chirágh-kush of the Persians and Or-mur of the Afghans), either deserted their own creeds for the more popular state religion, or, clinging to the faith of their forefathers, sunk to a state of servitude or dependance. There are still several Shíá clans amongst the different tribes of Patháns, and since the decline of Islám as a state power in these parts, they manage to maintain their position with greater security and freedom than before. With the Chamkani, it was different. He was a proscribed and persecuted heretic by both churches of Islám, and soon, for self-preservation, became a Sunni, though still retaining his former appellation.

CHAPTER XI.

THE GHILJI.

THE Ghiljai (plural Ghiljí) as he calls himself—Ghilzai, as strangers call him—is a numerous and widespread people, extending from Jalalabad in the east to Kaláti Ghilji in the west, and occupying the adjoining slopes and spurs of Sufed Koh, Suleman Koh, and Gul Koh (west of Ghazni). The Afghan traditions place their original settlements in the Kohi Kais or Koh Kásí, but there seems to be some doubt as to the whereabouts of this locality, some considering it to be on the Suleman range, and others on the Siyah-band range of the Ghor mountains. The latter, it would seem, is the more probable, as it was the scene of the romantic episode by which the Afghan genealogists account for the name.

The story runs to the effect that the second son of Kais (the great ancestral progenitor of the Afghan nationality), who was named Batan, was settled with his people on the Siyah-band range of the Ghor mountains—the Paropamisus of the ancients, the Hazarah of the moderns. It appears that they occupied the western hills of the range, and led a migratory life between the highlands in summer and lowlands in winter. Batan, the patriarch of the tribe, was noted for his piety and devotion, and for his earnest attachment to the new faith established in those parts. In consequence of his leading position and religious reputation, he was reverenced as a saint and honored with the title of Shekh.

During the reign of the Khàlif Walíd—towards the close of the first century of the Muhammadan era, and during the early part of the eighth of our own—an Arab army was sent from Baghdad for the conquest of Khúrásan and Ghor (a name the signification of which is "mountainous"). On its approach to the northern mountains of Ghor, which were at that time inhabited by Bani Isráíl and Bani Afghan, and other castaway tribes, one of the princes of the country, who, it appears, was himself of a refugee family, since many generations exiled from Persia, fled his retreat, and sought asylum with Shekh Batan, whose *tuman* or "tribal camp" was in some neighbouring mountain recesses. Batan, perceiving that the stranger was of noble birth, welcomed him to the hospitality and protection of his people, and took him into his own house as a member of the family. The stranger guest soon ingratiated himself with his hosts, and won the confidence of the chief, who always consulted him in the affairs of the tribe as if he were a member of it. In fact he was made quite at home, and treated with the fullest liberty and trust.

The Shekh had a daughter, whose name was Matto, a handsome maiden in the bloom of youth. In the simple manners and freedom of action that characterize life in camp, the inmates of the tent or booth were thrown much together in the routine of daily domestic life. Well, to cut a long story short—the guest and his host's daughter fell in love with each other, and carried on a clandestine amour with the natural consequences. The first signs were early discovered by the quick eye of the mother, who at once communicated her suspicions to the girl's father. The old Shekh—Afghan-like—was for summary punishment and the swift execution of both the guilty parties. But the mother, with keener perception and more far-seeing calculation, suggested the propriety of first ascertaining whether their guest—Shah Husen by name—really was of the royal descent he had represented himself to be, and whether the future of his prospects were as bright as he had colored them.

For this purpose a trusted domestic was despatched to the home in Northern Ghor, indicated by Shah Husen, to find out all about his family and antecedents. He duly returned with a favourable report, and even more than confirming all that Shah Husen had said of himself. On this, the parents, accepting the situation, hastily married the couple to avoid the imminent scandal. Shortly after these occurrences, Bíbí Matto presented Shah Husen with a son, whom the irate old Shekh, in allusion to the circumstances connected with his birth, named Ghalzoe—"son of a thief"—the father having stolen his daughter's honor. The name in time came to be used to distinguish the whole tribe, and by vulgar usage became changed to Ghilzai.

Such, in brief, is the Afghan account. It seems to point to an early mixture of the original Ghilji with some tribe of Ghor, perhaps of Persian descent, though the name Batan sounds of Indian origin (the Sanskrit name of the Brahman priests being Bata), and the title of Shekh being the one usually applied in India to converts from Brahmanism to Islám.

Bíbí Matto had a second son, who was named Ibrahím, continue the Afghan accounts, and he was surnamed *Loe*, or "Great," by his grandfather, on account of some act of infantile precocity. This name became corrupted into *Lodí*, and was adopted as the title of his descendants, who afterwards formed a considerable tribe, which, in the fifteenth century, furnished the Lodí dynasty of kings on the throne of Delhi. Such are the idle tales by which the Afghan historians attempt to account for the presence in their midst of a foreign race of whose antecedents they know nothing. That the Lodí and Súr kings of the house of Ghor, who reigned at Delhi as sovereigns of Hindustan, were of the Ghiljí race, there seems no reason to doubt, but that they were in any way connected by tribal affinity with the Afghan is by no means clear.

Besides the sons already mentioned, Bíbí Matto is said by the Afghan accounts to have borne Shah Husen a number of other sons, *viz.*, Túrán, Tolar, Búrán, and Polar. Here are names of quite a different stamp, and their character is maintained in the subdivisions of tribes springing from them in succeeding generations. Thus Túrán is divided into the clans of Tokhí and Hotak, whilst amongst those classed as sprung from Búrán are the Andar and Tarakí. All these names are distinctly of Turk origin, and the evidence of the Afghan accounts, such as they are, go to show that (even if there had been a prior immigration of some part of this Turk tribe) about the beginning of the eighth century of our era, when the Arabs were overruning Transoxiana—the country called Turán in contradistinction to Irán—with the sword and Kuran, certain Turk tribes, known by the name of Khilich or Khilichí, and said to be Christians of the Nestorian Church—at that time a flourishing patriarchate in both Western and Eastern Turkistan—emigrated from their native country and sought refuge in the inaccessible mountains of Ghor.

The word Khilich means a "sword," and Khilichí, a "swordsman," just as, according to the Turk custom of naming their tribes after some individual peculiarity or characteristic,—Cazzác or Cossack means a "robber;" Kirghiz or Cirghiz, a "wanderer;" Uzbak, an "independent;" Cara Calpac, a "black hat;" Kizil básh, "red head," &c. The Khilichí, when they entered Ghor, probably consisted only of the true Turk clans of Hotak, Tokhí, Andar, Tarakí, Tolar, and Polar (the last two of which are lost in the Afghan reckoning), and made good their settlement there by force of arms amongst a mixed population of Jews, Israelites, Afghans, Indians, and Persians. How long they stayed in Ghor is unknown, but it is probable that from their nomade habits of life, and the constant military expeditions of the Arabs through South-western Afghanistan at that period, they early moved forward, and finally settled in the country they now hold; that is, from a little to the east of Kalat-i-Ghiljí to Shalgar and Abistada to the south of Ghazni. The eastern part of this country, at the head waters of the Tarnak and Arghasán rivers, is a rich pasture tract in the summer season, whilst the open plain and steppe to the westward affords good winter quarters in the sheltered hollows of the undulating surface. This country was the first real and permanent settlement of the Ghiljí in Afghanistan, and during the early centuries of the Muhammadan era was known by the name of Túrán—probably, from the name of the combined clans—just as at the same period, the country to the south, including the present Peshín and Shál or Quetta, was called Búdha from the Budhists inhabiting it.

From Túrán, the Khilichí or Ghilji, it would appear, spread eastward to the rich pastures of the Sulemán range, till they possessed themselves of the western slopes up to the present Waziri and Kákar borders. And this extension was effected not so much by direct conquest, or actual overflow of their own tribal population, as by the absorption and assimilation of weaker and obscure clans whom they found upon their borders. And this view is supported by the change in name of the new clans successively enrolled under the name of the dominant one. Doubtless they included a variety of different races, and some of them were possibly of kindred stock, such as the Babur Ghiljí, who had been planted here in earlier invasions of Turk tribes from the north.

What the origin of these new clans was, whether they were conquered and converted Patháns, who became absorbed into the dominant tribe, and thus, by the mere force of numbers and other favouring circumstances of the period, gave them both their language and social code of laws; or whether they were kindred tribes of Turks imported by Sabaktakin (that is, the one called Sabak, as Alaptakin, the one called Alap, *takin* being a distinctive affix of the names of Turk slaves), the founder of the Turk Tatar (as distinguished from the Mughal or Mongal Tatar) dynasty at Ghazni, is not clearly ascertained. Without excluding the possibility of their increase by the occasional immigration of other kindred Turk clans from across the Oxus, it may be considered more probable that the increase in the clans of the Ghilji took place mostly by the absorption and adoption of subjugated native tribes. For we find several instances of Chaghatai Turk clans living in close proximity to the Ghilji, yet quite distinct from them, and entirely ignorant of any kindred connection with them. Such Turk clans are the Bayát about Ghazni and Herat, the Cárlúgh, Chung, and Mughal Turk (Yaka, Chirík-cha, &c.) of Balkh, &c. Such, also, are the Mongol and Chaghatai Turk clans of Mangal, Jájí, Jadrán, Khitáí, &c., who are settled about the Pewár and the head waters of the Kurram river, and who were brought to these situations on the invasions of Changhiz and Tymur—the Tatar scourges of the world during the thirteenth and fifteenth centuries. These clans, with the exception of the Jadrán, though they have almost entirely lost the typical physiognomy of their race, their mother-tongue, and, indeed, everything else but their names, which would connect them with their original stock, nevertheless hold themselves entirely distinct—political relations always excepted—from the Ghilji, who are their neighbours. The study of the history and origin of these obscure clans is a very important one, and interesting as well on its own merits, as yet it has hardly been even thought of.

The Ghilji of Afghanistan first come prominently into notice in the reign of Mahmúd of Ghazni, who employed them largely as soldiers in his numerous invasions of India for the conversion of the land to Islám. It is probable that the tribe in the course of these successive expeditions, which extended over a period of eighteen or twenty years, and were sometimes conducted by the route south of Sufed Koh, that is, by the Pewár and Gomal or Ghawailari routes, and sometimes by those to the north of that range, that is, by the Khybar, Abkhána, Hinduráj, &c., through Swat to Peshawar, enlarged their original borders by the conquest and colonization of the territories they now hold to the eastward of Ghazni, as far as the Suleman range and the valley of Jalalabad,—an operation the more easy to them by reason of their nomadic and military mode of life—a characteristic in their manners which still distinguishes this people from all the other races inhabiting Afghanistan.

As a race the Ghilji mix little with their neighbours, and indeed differ in many respects, both as to internal government and domestic customs, from the other races of Afghanistan. Those small sections of the people, who are settled in the plain, live in villages and follow agricultural pursuits; but the great majority of the tribe are pastoral in their habits of life, and migrate with the seasons from the lowlands to the highlands with their families and flocks, and easily portable black hair tents. They never settle in the cities, nor do they engage in the ordinary handicraft trades, but they manufacture carpets, felts, &c., for domestic use, from the wool and hair of their cattle. The pastoral clans are notoriously predatory in their habits, and continually at fued amongst themselves and with their neighbours. Physically they are a remarkably fine race, and in stature, courage, and strength of body are second to none in Afghanistan; but they are a very barbarous people, the pastoral clans especially, and in their wars excessively savage and vindictive.

Several of the Ghilji or Ghilzai clans are almost wholly engaged in the carrying-trade between India and Afghanistan and the northern states of Central Asia, and have been so for many centuries to the exclusion almost of all the other tribes of the country. The principal clans employed in this great carrying-trade are the Níází, Násar, Kharotí, and, to some extent, the Sulemánkhel. From the nature of their occupation they are collectively styled, or individually so far as that goes, Povinda and Lawáni, or Loháni. These terms, it appears, are derived from the Persian words *parwinda*, a "bale of merchandise," and *rawání*, a "traveller."

Their principal routes to India are by the Ghawailari or Gomal and the Zhob passes, and they fight their way backwards and forwards every journey in enormous caravans of the combined clans, disposed in regular military order against the attacks of the Waziri and Kákar, through whose territories they pass. The several clans travel with their families and flocks and dependents, as well as with their merchandize, and the whole together form a vast assemblage, numbering many thousands of fighting men and beasts of burden, besides the families and flocks. They assemble in autumn in the plains of Zurmat and Gardez and Kattawáz to the east of Ghazni, and, after making good their way through the passes to the Deraját, they leave their families and flocks to pasture there, whilst a portion of each clan goes on into India with the merchandize. These enterprising merchants carry their long files of camels straight across country to Delhi, whence they disperse by rail or road to the principal cities of India, and always arrange so as to return to their families in the Deraját early in the spring for the homeward journey. They bring down various productions of their own country, such as fruits, madder, asafœtida, wool and woollen fabrics, furs, drugs, &c., together with horses, raw silk, shawl, wool, &c., from Bukhara. And they take back cotton piece-goods, chintzes, broadcloth, velvet, &c., of English manufacture, together with tea, spices, metals, and variety of other articles, such as brocades, silks, and muslins, &c., of Indian manufacture.

During the cold weather, the Povinda is to be seen in most of the larger cities of India, and at once attracts attention in the crowds of the bazar by his thorough strangeness of appearance and rude independence of manner. His loose, untidy dress, generally in a state of dirt beyond the washerman's cure, and often covered with a shaggy sheep-skin coat, travel-stained and sweat-begrimed to an extent that proclaims the presence of the wearer to the nostrils though he be out of sight in the crowd; his long unkempt and frayed locks, loosely held together by some careless twists of a coarse cotton turban, soiled to the last degree, if not tattered also, add to the wildness of his unwashed and weather-worn features; whilst his loud voice and rough manners complete the barbarian he is proud to pass for. Such is the common Povinda and caravan driver as seen in the bazar. There are others of superior stamp, wealthy merchants, or well-to-do traders, who drop the barbarian rôle, and appear in decent flowing robes, with capacious and carefully adjusted turbans, well modulated voices, manners studiedly polite, and a keenness for business second to none. But these are the few, and they mix not with the public throng.

These Povinda clans, though classed as subdivisions of the Ghilji people, differ from them in one or two important respects. The Kharoti and Násir, for example, differ markedly in features, complexion, and stature from the Sulemánkhel and Túrán clans, and, moreover, keep a good deal to themselves in their internal clan government; whilst their hereditary occupation, as travelling merchants for a long course of centuries, without any other clans of the tribe joining them in it, is a remarkable fact, and, with the other circumstances stated, would seem to indicate a difference of origin.

Of the history of the Ghilji as a distinct people in Afghanistan little or nothing is known till the beginning of last century, when they revolted against the Persian Governor of Kandahar. The Persians, it appears, had for several years been most oppressive in their rule over the people of this province, and the Ghilji sent numerous petitions to the court of Ispahan praying for a removal of their grievances. These petitions receiving no attention, the Ghilji deputed one of their chief men, named Mír Vais, or Wais, to lay their complaints before the Shah, and obtain for them some redress for the sufferings they groaned under. The mission of Mír Vais proved unsuccessful, but his journey was not altogether without advantage, for his residence at the Shah's court opened his eyes to the weakness of the government and the venality of its officers.

Mír Vais returned to Kandahar by way of Mecca, the pilgrimage to the sacred shrines of which city added the title of Haji to his name, and much increased his influence amongst his countrymen ; and, immediately on his arrival at home, he set to work to raise the people in revolt. The rising proved successful, the Persian Governor was slain, his troops were defeated and dispersed, and Mír Vais became independent ruler of Kandahar. He reigned eight years, during which he repulsed three Persian armies sent against him, and died in 1715 A.D., leaving the government to his son and successor Mahmúd. The repeated failures of the Persian government to recover their authority at Kandahar, encouraged Mahmúd to assume the offensive, aud in 1720 he invaded Persia by way of Kirman, but was signally defeated and driven back by the Governor of that province.

Two years later, however, he renewed the attempt with a larger and better equipped army, and with complete success. He overran the whole of Southern Persia, taking city after city, and spreading terror and devastation wherever he went, till, at the end of the second year's campaign, he became master of Ispahan, the Persian sovereign, Shah Husen, abdicating the throne and surrendering his capital to the conqueror. Flushed with his rapid and great successes, the pride and ambition of Mahmúd increased, and giving way to unbridled excesses of all kinds, he soon became an insane and bloody savage.

His cruelties and unreasonable despotism at length became intolerable to his own chiefs, who assassinated him, and put his nephew, Mír Ashraf, on the throne in his place. He had not long enjoyed the government when he had to face a better man, a soldier of fortune, who was soon to make himself of world-wide repute as a great conqueror. This was Nadir, a Turkman highwayman by birth and occupation, who entered the service of Tamasp, the heir of Shah Husen, as general of his army. As soon as Nadír took the field Ashraf boldly advanced to meet him, but was completely defeated. The Ghilji, however, did not give up the game as lost, but vigorously maintained the contest for some years, till, finally, having sustained a succession of crushing defeats, his heterogeneous and rabble army was either destroyed or dispersed, and he himself forced to flee the country with only three or four personal attendants. He took the way to Kandahar by Sistan, and was murdered in that district by a petty Baloch chief. And thus ended the Ghilji rule in Persia, after a term of only seven years; but it was a period of terror and savagery, and sufficed to steep the country in the blood of its inhabitants, and to overspread its surface with desolation and ruin.

After he had cleared Persia of the Ghilji invaders and secured his successes against the Russians and the Turks, Nadír assumed the crown himself, and then set out on his conquest of India. In 1738, after a siege of a year and-a-half, during which he devasted the districts around, he took the strong city of Kandahar and razed it to the ground. He then proceeded to Kabul and India, and took a strong contingent of Ghiljí troops along with his army. At Kabul he left as *chandaul*, or "rear guard," a detachment of twelve thousand of his Kizilbash (so named from the red caps they wore), or Mughal Persian troops. After the death of Nadír they remained at Kabul as a military colony, and their descendants still occupy a distinct quarter of the city, which is called Chandaul. These Kizilbash hold their own ground here as a distinct Persian community of the Shiá persuasion against the native population of the Sunni profession. They constitute an important element in the general population of the city, and exercise a considerable influence in its local politics. Owing to their isolated position and antagonism to the native population, they are favourably inclined to the British authority.

On the death of Nadír Shah and the rise of the Durraní to the independent sovereignty of Afghanistan, the Ghilji were bought over by Ahmad Shah, and acquiesced in his elevation to the throne. On the death of the Abdáli king, however, their long suppressed discontent burst out, and, impatient of their position as a subordinate race in the seat of their recent supremacy, they openly contested the sovereignty against his successor, the Shah Tymur. The struggle was continued in a desultory and intermittent manner for many years, till, finally, the Ghilji power was crushed by Shah Zamán in the early part of the present century by a decisive battle fought in 1809 at Jaldak near Kalat-i-Ghilzi.

Since that time—coeval with the establishment for the first time of diplomatic relations between the Governments of India and Afghanistan—the Ghilji have made no effort to recover their lost position, or to attain to the dominant authority in the country; but they have, in consequence, by no means sunk into insignificance. On the contrary they have maintained a considerable amount of tribal independence, and have uniformly exercised a very powerful influence in the councils of the Durrani rulers, so far, at least, as concerns the guidance of state affairs. Our own experience of this people on each occasion of our contact with them in Afghanistan has been that of unmitigated hostility and the deepest treachery; not acting by themselves alone, but in concert with the Durrani.

The trouble they gave us in harassing our communications between Kabul and Kandahar during our occupation of the country in 1839-42, the unrelenting ferocity of their attacks upon our defenceless and retreating army in 1842, and their persistent opposition to our avenging force later in the same year upon the Khybar route, are all matters of history, and need not be here further referred to. But with all this against them, the Ghilji is not an implacable foe to us, and by judicious management can be converted into a very useful friend.

CHAPTER XII.

THE TAJIK.

THE TAJIK, or, as he is frequently called, the Parsiwan, constitute a numerous and widely spread portion of the inhabitants of Afghanistan, from whom they differ in language, internal government, and manners and customs. They are the representatives of the ancient Persian inhabitants of the country, as the Afghans are of its ancient Indian inhabitants. It would appear that as the Afghans (whose true home and seat are in the Kandahar and Arghandáb valleys) mixed and intermarried with the Indian people whom they conquered, and gave their name to the mixed race, so the Arabs, who did the same with the Persian people whom they conquered, left their name as the national designation of their mixed posterity,—that is, the name by which they were called by the Persians. Where the Arab progenitors were Sayyids, that is descendants of the Khalif Ali, son-in-law of Muhammad, they gave their own designation to the tribes sprung from them. There are several Sayyid tribes in Afghanistan, the principal being the Wardak and Ushturani. The term Tajik, it is said, is derived from the ancient Persian name for the Arab. The ancient Persian writers distinguishing their hereditary enemies on the north and south respectively by the terms Turk and Táz or Táj. And hence it is that the term Táz applied to the Arab only in Persia; and every thing connected with him, or proceeding from him, was called by the Persians Tázi or Tázik, which are the same as Tájí or Tájik. In course of time, it seems these terms became restricted to designate things of Arab origin in Persia in contradistinction to the pure and native article. Thus an Arab settling in the country, and not intermarrying with its people, retained his proper national title through successive generations. But the Arab intermarrying with the people of the country lost his proper nationality, and, in the succeeding generations, was called Tájik by the Persians. An imported Arab horse or dog, &c., was not called Tazi but Arabi. Their offspring, however, from a Persian mare or bitch received the name of Tází, and were no longer called Arabi. By some, however, the term is said to signify "Persian," and there is also reason to believe that the Táochi of the Chinese is the same word as the modern Tájik. If so, and this latter appears to be the correct version, the former explanation must be rejected, and Tájik be held to be merely the ancient name for the Persian cultivator or peasant. The word, in fact, being a Persian one, is restricted to the territories which formerly owned the Persian sovereignty. Hence its absence from India, and its presence in Turkistan. The Tájik extend all over the plain country of Afghanistan from Herat to the Khybar and from Kandahar to the Oxus, and even into Kashghar. The name is applied nowadays in a very loose way, and is made to include all the Persian-speaking people of the country who are not either Hazarah, Afghan, or Sayyid. Thus the Indian races on the southern slopes of Hindu Kush, who have been converted to Muhammadanism and speak Persian (as well as to some extent their native dialects), are commonly called Tájik. The term is also applied to the representatives of the ancient Persian inhabitants of Badakhshan and its inaccessible mountain glens.

These people are divided into distinct communities, who have for long centuries maintained their independence, though they are now nominally subjects of the Kabul Government. They are professedly Musalmáns of either the Sunni or Shia sect, claim to be descendants of Alexander the Great and his Greek soldiers, differ in appearance, as well as in some of their manners and customs, from the Tájiks of the plain country, and speak different dialects of Persian, which are supposed to be offshoots of the ancient Pahlaví. They are known as the Badakhshí, the Wákhí, the Shughní, the Roshání, &c., of Badakhshán, Wakhán, Shughnán, &c., and in this respect differ from the Tájik of the plains, who has no such subdivisional distinctions, but is simply a Tájik, whether of Herat, Kandahar, Kabul, or elsewhere. Further, the Tajik has no divisions into *Khel* and *Zai*, as have the Afghan, the Ghilzi and the Pathán. The terms *Khel* and *Zai*, added to a proper name, signify the "association" or "descendants" sprung from that individual, but they do not necessarily imply that the members of the association, or the descendants, are the actual offspring of his own loins. The word *Khel* is Arabic, and signifies a "troop" (especially of horse), "company," "party," &c. The suffix *zai* is Persian, and means literally "born of," but is commonly used in the same sense as *Khel*, as Músazai or Músakhel, the "offspring" or "party" of Moses. A very recent illustration of the use of these terms is found in the formation of two factions at Kabul, shortly after the establishment of our envoy there, a few months ago. The party in favour of the British alliance being called Cavagnarízai, and those opposed to it, Yácúbzai. The suffix *khel* might have been used with equal propriety, but euphony gives the preference to the other. These divisions in fact correspond to the Got and Sakha of the Rájpút peoples. Amongst the Tájiks are some agricultural communities who are called Dihwár in the west of Afghanistan, and Dihgán or Dihcán in the eastern provinces. They represent, it would appear, the Dahæ of the ancient Greek writers, and are merely rustics or villagers, as the above Persian words imply; though the ancient Scythian tribe of the Dasæ or Dahæ were a numerous and powerful people in their day. As a race the Tájiks of the plains are a handsome people, of tall stature, and robust frames. They are of a peaceable disposition, industrious, and frugal in their habits, and fond of social gatherings and amusements. They occupy a subordinate and, to some extent, servile position amongst the inhabitants of the country, and have no voice in its government or politics. In the rural districts they are entirely devoted to agriculture and gardening, either settled in village communities of their own, or scattered about as farm servants, gardeners, &c. In the towns and cities they furnish the several industrial and mechanical trades with their handicraftsmen, act as shopkeepers, petty traders, and merchants of substance and position. The accountants, secretaries, and overseers in public offices and private establishments are almost wholly recruited from their ranks, and they enjoy a high reputation for their intelligence, fidelity, and industry. They freely take service as household domestics or personal attendants, and are esteemed for their activity, diligence, and general tidiness. They rarely engage in military service, though some of them occupy high positions in the army of the Amir. They possess naturally many estimable qualities, but, being a subject and down-trodden people, they are very suspicious of their rulers, and meet force by deception. In intelligence, sobriety, industry, and fidelity to just masters, they surpass all the other inhabitants of the country, and they are, moreover, the best disposed towards the British Government. In this last respect they are in the same category as the Kizilbash colony of Kabul, the Hazarah under the Durrani rule, and the mercantile and trading community throughout the country. In fact, with the exception of the Ghilzi, who are semi-independent, and, to some considerable extent, participators in the government and direction of the policy of the country, and the Pathán, who are almost wholly independent and know nothing of any ruler, the Durrani or Afghan is our only real and implacable enemy, and it is astonishing how, through our own countenance and support of his authority, he has been able so successfully to embitter and stir up the hatred of the other races towards us, for he himself is detested and feared by all classes of the people.

CHAPTER XIII.

THE HAZARAH.

THIS people differ entirely from all the other races of Afghanistan, and occupy a very extensive area of country, extending from the borders of Kabul and Ghazni to those of Herat in one direction, and from the vicinity of Kandahar to that of Balkh in the other. They hold, in fact, all the country which formed the Paropamisus of the ancients, and in their possession of it are isolated from all the other peoples of Afghanistan, with whom they are in contact only where their borders march together. This region is mountainous throughout, and for the most part the soil is poor. But it contains many fertile and populous valleys, and is the source of several important rivers, the Arghandáb and Helmand, the Harirúd or Herat river, and the Murghab or river of Marv. It is formed by the two great western prolongations of the Hindu Kush, which are separated from each other by the valley of the Harirúd, and is divided into Ghurjistan or Sufedband on the north, and Ghor or Siyah-band on the south; whilst the point on the east, whence the two ranges start from Hindu Kush, is the Ghor-band of Bamian.

The interior of this country is entirely unknown to Europeans, but we know from history that in former times it was a highly populous region, and took the famous conqueror Changhiz Khan a full decade to subdue and devastate. In his time it abounded in strong fortified places held by a population mostly of Persian race. The ruins of these mountain castles still exist in all parts of the country, and are described by the present inhabitants as wonderful structures perched on inaccessible peaks, the works of the genii and not of men, so solid and so vast are the walls and buildings still left amongst the deserted ruins. There are also numerous ruins of Budhist buildings in the eastern parts of the country, and large quantities of coins—mostly of the Greek Bactrian Kings—are found in them.

Regarding the ethnic affiliation of the Hazarah people there can be no doubt, their features and forms declaring them distinctly to be Tatar of the Mongol division. But little or nothing appears to be known for certain regarding their history and settlement in these parts, and they seem to have no traditions on tho subject themselves. The name too by which they are now known affords no clue, as it is not a native one, but of foreign derivation. The general idea regarding the origin of the word Hazarah is that it is derived from the Persian word *hazár*, "a thousand," and was applied to these people by their neighbours, in consequence of their having been planted here as military colonists in detachments of a thousand fighting men each by Changhiz Khan in the first quarter of the thirteenth century. It is said that Changhiz Khan left ten such detachments here, nine of them in the Hazarah of Kabul, and the tenth in the Hazarah of Paklí to the east of the Indus. This last, it would seem, was an outpost only whilst Changhiz wintered in Swat prior to his return to Tamghaj, and pending the Indian king's reply to his request for a passage to that country through India.

Amongst themselves this people never use the term Hazarah as their national appellation, and yet they have no name for their people as a nation. They are only known amongst themselves by the names of their several principal tribes and the clans subordinate to them respectively. Thus they are either Jághúrí or Bihsúd, or Dáhí Zangí, or Dáhí Kundí, or Gaur, &c., as the case may be. With respect to the two last named, the term Dáhí or Deh, as it is usually written by us, would seem to be a national appellation, and may be perhaps a trace of the Dahæ of Transoxiana, who at first fought with and then coalesced with the Saka in their invasion of this region about the time of the Christian era. There are other Hazarah tribes with the same prefix, as the Dáhí Ráwád, Dáhi Chopán Dáhyá, &c.; and amongst foreigners they seldom call themselves Hazarah, but generally Kabuli, and sometimes Ghilji or Aoghan. They acknowledge the Cháraymác, Jamshedí, Firozkohi, Tymúní, and other Tatar tribes in the western parts of the country as kindred, but have no very intimate relations with them. With the exception of a few Turki words, they have entirely lost their mother tongue and adopted in its place the Persian language of the thirteenth century, and with it the national form of religion of that people, namely, the Shíá doctrine of Islám. This is the case with the eastern tribes throughout, though some towards the north and west of the country are of the Sunni sect.

Whether the current explanation regarding the meaning and the application of the term Hazarah, as above expressed, meets the requirements of the case, is a doubtful question. In its favour is the fact of a district to the east of the Indus bearing the name of Hazarah, because it was held by one of the ten divisions of the Mongol troops before referred to, as well as the fact of the existence of the name Hazroh on the road to the Indus and not far from Attock, and of Hazrah on the road to Kabul from Kurram, and not far from the now celebrated Shaturgardan. Both these latter, being strategical points on the approaches to Kabul from the eastward, might well have been occupied by the troops of Changhiz, and thus received their names. On the other hand is the supposition of the country now called Hazarah being—under the form of Arsareth—the same as that alluded to by Esdras as the place of refuge of the captive Israelites after their escape from Persia,—a form which might easily be changed to the word now in use.

Very little is known of the manners and customs of this Tatar people. They are said, however, to be a simple-minded people, and very much in the hands of their priests. They are for the most part entirely illiterate, are governed by tribal and clan chiefs, whose authority over their people is absolute; and they are generally very poor and hardy. Many thousands of them come down to the Panjab every cold season in search of labour either on the roads, or as well-sinkers, wall-builders, &c. In their own country they have the reputation of being a brave and hardy race, and amongst the Afghans they are considered a faithful, industrious, and intelligent people as servants. Many thousands of them find employment at Kabul and Ghazni and Kandahar during the winter months as labourers—in the two former cities mainly in removing the snow from the house-tops and streets. In consequence of their being heretics, the Sunni Afghans hold them in slavery, and in most of the larger towns the servant-maids are purchased slaves of this people.

As a race the Hazarah are irreconcilably hostile to the Afghan, and they have always shown a good disposition towards us on the several occasions of our military operations in Afghanistan. The independent tribes in the interior, who have hitherto baffled the attempts of the Kabul Government to reduce them to subjection, are described as a very brave people, with many of the warlike characteristics of the Goorkha. In fact they may very properly be considered as the Goorkha of the west, for they are of the same race, and in physiognomy there is no difference between them, the Hazarah being of fairer complexion only. Of the numbers of this people nothing is known for certain, though they are roughly reckoned at one hundred and twenty thousand houses, exclusive of the Chár-aymác and western tribes. For us, in our new relations with Afghanistan, this people has a special and very important interest. With good management they may be entirely attached to us and our interests, and are capable of being converted into a very powerful advance-guard of our military position in the country.

Such is a very brief account of the principal races inhabiting Afghanistan. Their diversity of origin, different traditions and manners, and antagonistic interests explain how it is that no firm and consolidated government has been able to maintain itself in peace and security so long as the authority rested with one of them without the support of a foreign paramount power. The study of these different peoples is of itself most useful and interesting and of the first importance in view to their ere long becoming subjects of the British Empire—a lot they themselves are far from unwilling as a whole to accept.

INDEX.